OBEDIENCE

The Daring and Determined Way to it

Pastor Bim Folayan

WESTBOW®
PRESS
A DIVISION OF THOMAS NELSON
& ZONDERVAN

Unless otherwise indicated, all Scripture quotations are taken from the King James Version of the Bible.

Keys for other Bible translations used in this book:
AMP—The Amplified Bible
CEB—Common English Bible
CEV—Contemporary English Version
NCV—New Century Version
NIV—New International Version
NKJV—New King James Version
NLT—New Living Translation
TLB—The Living Bible

WestBow Press books may be ordered through booksellers or by contacting:

WestBow Press
A Division of Thomas Nelson & Zondervan
1663 Liberty Drive
Bloomington, IN 47403
www.westbowpress.com
1 (866) 928-1240

ISBN: 978-1-4908-1117-8 (sc)
ISBN: 978-1-4908-1119-2 (hc)
ISBN: 978-1-4908-1118-5 (e)

Library of Congress Control Number: 2013918383

Printed in the United States of America.

WestBow Press rev. date: 1/30/2014

Table of Contents

PHRASE HIGHLIGHTS FOR EACH CHAPTER

Chapter One Highlight

To obey is not to be obstinate but to be yielded to God so we are not obsolete.

Chapter Two Highlight

When we act at the right moment we access Godly results for making the right move.

Chapter Three Highlight

Depend on God's capability and not your capacity, His ability and not your agility, His facility and not your anxiety.

Chapter Four Highlight

The prize that follows obedience outweighs the price.

DEDICATION

To the glory of God,
to the partners
and friends of the ministry.

As you walk along in God's plan
With your hand in God's Hand
You will band in God's brand.
Bim Folayan
March 2010

Introduction

Obedience, from the word obey means to correspond in action, to conform, to comply with, to do as told or as instructed, to act upon and carry out. Our obedience to God fulfills divine purpose.

Yielding and living in line with God paves divine way for rewarding life's journey.

It is only when life's journey is made in relation and response to The True Wise Guide, in the Hands of life's Designer, that fulfilling steps are guaranteed.

This book is a result of obedience. Indeed obedience makes things happen. Let reading this book motivate you in making things God has said to you happen!

Abraham's Blessings

"That in blessing I will bless thee, and in multiplying I will multiply thy seed as the stars of the heaven, and as the sand which is upon the sea shore; and thy seed shall possess the gate of his enemies; And in thy seed shall all the nations of the earth be blessed; <u>because thou hast obeyed my voice.</u>"

Genesis 22:17-18

Chapter 1

In Line, In Form and In Tune

"For all those things hath mine hand made, and all those things have been, saith the Lord: but to this man will I look, even to him that is poor and of a contrite spirit, and trembleth at my word."
Isaiah 66:2

Man has a maker, and his Maker is God, who designed each man with an intention for His particular purpose. No man in life is an accident; with God, there is a reason for every man. God, man's Designer, had a purpose for His creation and would have His creation operate according to His plan and direction through compliance (obedience), so that the aim of creation can be established. As His creation, we thrive and flourish by His Word.

Matthew 4:4 says *"But he answered and said, it is written, Man shall not live by bread alone, but by every word that proceedeth out of the mouth of God."*

Obedience, from the word *obey,* means to comply with, to submit to, to act upon, to carry out orders or instructions and adhere to them. To be obedient is to keep in observance to order, instructions, and respect for authority, etc. Obedience involves aligning with God's plan and purposes, keeping a focus on what is to be done, and maintaining a composure through conforming to the plan of God, regardless of any circumstance, until the will of God is done. It involves making sacrificial wise choices. Our love for God must compel us to obey Him. "Let us hear the conclusion of the whole matter: *Fear God, and keep his commandments:* **for this is the whole duty of man**" (Ecclesiastics 12:13).

Obedience makes God's word effective in our lives. Obeying God gives us the advantage if we walk in line, in form, and in tune with God in fulfilling His intent for our lives as individuals. Our spirits must be constantly tuned to God, willing and ready to respond in line with God's will. Apostle Paul testifies in Hebrews 6:5 that he has tasted the good

Word of God. It is by doing God's Word, written for us or spoken to us, that we can derive its taste and partake of its benefit.

Obedience is not obedience unless it is done with precision. Noah worked with precision to get God's perfect result. He obeyed God in exactness. By working with precision, Noah was accurate and in line with instructions given. When we do not follow God's word precisely, we disobey. Disobedience to God's Word is resistance and opposition to God's plan, and where this is the case, an individual is exposed and vulnerable. God's Word guides and guards us in divine plan and protection. For safety, God's Word must have the final say in our lives, for He is the Creator and Owner of all things, inclusive of us, so His Word must be the final arbiter. To be disobedient to God amounts to pride because the individual is not surrendering, submitting, or succumbing to His will. The Bible says in James 4:6 that God resist the proud which means to be opposed by Him, implying danger and failure. To the humble, the Bible says God grants more grace and ability because of the humble man's willingness and responsiveness. To the humble, God gives enablement because he is keen to respond.

Obedience to God amounts to success. Where there is disobedience to God, there is demonstration of lack of faith in Him; for faith is backed up by action. Our faith indicates our trust, confidence, dependency, and reliance on God. The Bible says in Ephesians 2:10 that *"we are His workmanship, created in Christ Jesus unto good works,* **which God hath before ordained that we should walk in them.***"*

Without faith, we do not please God (Hebrews 11:6). If we have faith and really do love God, as we say, then we will obey and do His will, and our acts of obedience (tough or easy) will translate into solutions or progress worked together for our own good (Romans. 8:28). By this, we attain God's expected end for our lives and the purpose for our being. Obedience translates to power and life because we are in adherence to the will and direction of God our Father who assures us of His guidance. Proverbs 6:23 states, *"For the commandment is a lamp; and the law is light; and reproofs of instruction are the way of life."*

Determined obedience is dogged; it does not consider anything above God's instruction. It considers the end result and not the means or process. When our obedience is resolute, we operate by faith and not by sight. (2 Corinthians 5:7).

In Acts 9:10-17, Ananias had to obey the instruction from God to go and meet Saul despite Saul's dreadful reputation and threats to Christians at the time. Though tough, Ananias nonetheless obeyed the Lord and went to Saul as instructed, despite what would be said of his association with a notorious sinner, coupled with the risk of his own life. Such obedience signifies complete surrender in honour to God.

The Word of God gives us clear-cut instructions, such as loving the Lord with all our hearts and souls (Matthew 22:37) that keeps us in fulfillment. On the other hand, to work against divine instruction and will is to fail.

The Bible says in Ephesians 1:11 *"In whom also we have obtained an inheritance, being predestinated according to the purpose of him who worketh all things after the counsel of his own will."* To obey God is to be in sync with the Creator. Products are made to function according to the manufacturers' intention and its instruction manual. As a product has its manual to guide for it to function efficiently and maximally, so has God, our Manufacturer, given His Word, both written and spoken to guide us into fulfillment. We as His products must function according to His Word in the Manual the Bible to guide us.

To function contrary to manual and guidelines is to malfunction. Such products fail and forfeit manufacturer's intention, idea or purpose. Disobedience therefore means failing. Obeying God's Word keeps us in line with God. The Holy Spirit has also been given to guide and direct the believer (John 16:13).

Ephesians 2:10(CEB) says, *"Instead, we are God's accomplishment, created in Christ Jesus to do good things. God planned for these good things to be the way that we live our lives."*

Obedience synchronizes us with God's pre-ordained order for each individual and paves way through divine destiny in God.

To obey God and His Word guarantees safe life journey. It involves walking and working according to God's plan and purpose for us with the ultimate goal of an 'expected end'. Only those who obey God are guaranteed safety (Psalm 91:1). They are secure and safe because the Word of God that they obey gives them protection and security (Proverbs 18:10). Since they dwell within the will of The All-knowing God, listening and responding to His will, they are safe. By their obedience, they heed to His warnings of danger. They are the ones dependent on God for their well-being, who have made His Word their mainstay.

Obedience involves focusing and concentrating on what God wants us to do rather than what we want to do. This is in order that we may be who He created us to be as we walk in the path of His will for us. The Word of God in Proverbs 23:26 say, *"My son, give me thine heart, and let thine eyes observe my ways."* We therefore must be obedient, as by-product of being God-inspired.

Proverbs 3:5-6 states, *"Trust in the Lord with all thine heart, and lean not unto thine own understanding. 6. In all thy ways acknowledge Him, and He shall direct thy paths."*

God directs us through His Word, guiding us through the Holy Spirit on what to do by communicating His intent to our spirits. John 16:13 states, *"Howbeit when he, the Spirit of truth, is come, he will guide you into all truth: for he shall not speak of himself; but whatsoever he shall hear, that shall he speak: and he will shew you things to come."*

David could confidently boast of God's presence, provision, sustenance, protection, guidance, and guardianship because he submitted to God's leading. Psalm 23:3–4 says, *"He leadeth me in the paths of righteousness for his name's sake. Yea, though I walk through the valley of the shadow of death, I will fear no evil: for thou art with me; thy rod and thy staff they comfort me."*

It is only a man who is fully submitted to God who would speak this way. The Bible talks about bringing into captivity every thought to the obedience of Christ. In 2 Corinthians 10:5-6 it says, *"Casting down imaginations, and every high thing that exalteth itself against the knowledge of God, and bringing into captivity every thought to the obedience of Christ; 6.And having in a readiness to revenge all disobedience, when your obedience is fulfilled."*

Israel, when they requested a king, got the following warning through the prophet Samuel in order for them to remain in God's will: *"If ye will fear the Lord, and serve him, and obey his voice, and not rebel against the commandment of the Lord, then shall both ye and also the king that reigneth over you continue following the Lord your God: 15. But if ye will not obey the voice of the Lord, but rebel against the commandment of the Lord, then shall the hand of the Lord be against you, as it was against your fathers."* (1 Samuel 12:14-15). In essence, to remain in God, we must obey Him.

In Acts 10:9-48 we see how Peter's obedience in the face of a difficult situation preserved Cornelius and his household. Obedience preserves us in the will of the Father while disobedience destroys –remember Lot's wife! The instruction Peter received was daunting and did not add up; it was in conflict with the tradition, culture, and norms of the Jews. As believers in Christ are to comply with God above tradition or man's perception of us, for their acceptance will not make us fit for the Master's use.

For obedience to be effective, we must overlook all circumstance and give God's will first place. In Acts 11:2-12, we see Peter adhere to God's will at the risk of being alienated. In obedience, he focused on the will of the Father. His response extended the opportunity of salvation to the Gentiles. Obedience to God preserves.

David in determination to be obedient, said in Psalm 119:11, *"Thy word have I hid in mine heart, that I might not sin against thee."* To disobey God is to sin. Obedience keeps us walking in The Manufacturer's original plan and intention, and as such, not at variance. We must be determined to conform and not contradict our Maker's instruction, following His written Word for us (The Bible, our Manual), or His spoken Word as directed and revealed by His Spirit to our spirits. In Joshua 7:11-12 we see that when we operate contrary to God's intention or purpose, not functioning according to His intention, we allow failure and its consequence.

Our obedience is an act of devotion to God. David said in Psalm 25:5, *"Lead me in thy truth, and teach me: for thou art the God of my salvation; on thee do I wait all the day."* Obeying God updates and develops us in His will for our individual fulfillment. By obedience we are training ourselves for life of dominion and control that will enable us to be over in life and not otherwise dominated by pleasurable hindering factors (Proverbs 14:12). As we give ourselves to obedience, yielding to God's directions, obeying to do the easy and the not so easy ones, the convenient and the inconvenient, we are building our lives and shaping our future in line with the Maker's perfect design. God is good and His intentions are always good. Jeremiah 29:11 says, *"For I know the thoughts that I think toward you, saith the Lord, thoughts of peace, and not of evil, to give you an expected end"*. He will guide us according to the path of life ordained for us by moulding us in obedience in various situations.

Psalm 84:11-12 says, *"For the Lord God is a sun and shield: the Lord will give grace and glory: no good thing will he withhold from them that walk uprightly.12 O Lord of hosts, blessed is the man that trusteth in thee."* When we honour God by responding to His Word, He gives grace to the doer.

I can recount many situations of responding to God by having to do specific things that I would have never considered doing. Though I found some of them odd, but having settled it that God's Word will always have the final say, I automatically complied. God is faithful! Through many daunting and challenging tasks, He has always been faithful seeing me through.

I depended on Him wholly through these tasks while relying and trusting Him each step of the way. There is great satisfaction in obeying the Lord; every act of obedience is opportunity for His blessing. In doing as The Lord instructs and also in communing with Him, He loads me with assuring scripture(s) to help me carry me through the tasks (Psalm 68:19). From these Scriptures, I draw strength accompanied with the joy and satisfaction of being able to comply with God's will.

Stage by stage the task gets done (2 Corinthians 3:18) and I discover that the act of obedience was for my good. What we must remember at all times is that God knows better than we do. So all we need is to trust and rely on Him absolutely and confidently. If we say we love God, then we must trust Him and obey Him as disobedience is a sign of lack of trust. Obedience results in knowledge and wisdom for us. Proverbs 21:11 says, *"...when the wise is instructed, he receiveth knowledge."* This is the way we acquire wisdom and success in life when we are fully submitted to God's purpose. God's Word is wisdom, which we attain when we carry out His Word. Proverbs 13:18 says, *"Poverty and shame shall be to him that refuseth instruction: but he that regardeth reproof shall be honoured."*

God speaks to His children through His written Word (2 Timothy 3:16) and to our spirits which we developed through fellowship (Psalm 16:11). As our corresponding action backs up God's direction received (Acts 8:29-30), the more we will attain the wisdom and progress that gives us the advantage in life (Proverbs 4:20-23). As God's children, the expectation is that we are obedient (1 Peter

1:14) and that our lives are fashioned after God and His will in order that we demonstrate His glory (1 Peter 2:9). As we live obedient to God's will, His Word directs us, giving us the divine advantage and insight into reality. By this we live secured and we are preserved in our relationship with God (John 10:27-28).

The ministry I run today is a product of obedience. Very important in the life of Christians is the fear of God which motivates us to do God's will. Constantly acknowledging the supremacy of God in reverential fear is the first step to fulfilling destiny. When we settle it in our hearts that God has the final say, it will make us submissive to His will. David said in Psalm 143:10 (NIV), *"Teach me to do your will, for you are my God; may your good Spirit lead me on level ground.* The Bible says in John 4:24 that God is a Spirit and those who worship Him must do so in the spirit, expecting that our spirits over our flesh must be yielded to Him.

The believer in Christ has been made alive to God and the promise of the Father is that he will not be left comfortless. This is the reason we have the person of the Holy Spirit to lead us in God's plan and purpose for our lives. The Bible says the Holy Spirit will not speak of Himself but whatever the Father says or reveals (John 16:13-14). So, by the Spirit of God leading us in divine direction and by His written Word (the Scripture), we are able to keep the right path for us through life. (Psalm 16:11).

In 2006, a particularly busy year for me, by the Spirit of God I received instruction to embark on a specific project outside my locality which I ordinarily would not have considered, but I already have it resolved to submit to God rather than disobey (sin). I accepted the additional task, trusting that God is my sufficiency.

I embarked on the project headlong and God began to give me insights and revelations which I simply embraced. I read His Word for more acquaintance, ensuring I walked along in His directions.

Having been raised to give honour to authority, the Authority of God being the ultimate was therefore not to be compromised at all. By the reason of close relationship nurtured with God, I simply just accessed strength, courage and enablement for the task.

The more I read His Word in the Bible, the more I operated in the efficacy and inspiration derived from it (2 Timothy 3:16-17). By confidence derived from His words that came to me, I journeyed through the task; I gave up my plans for His plans. Each step of the way, things got clearer as I gained understanding but not necessarily easier. Nonetheless, I received assuring comfort (John 14:18) through the tasks. I held on to Romans 8:28 which says, *"And we know that all things work together for good to them that love God, to them who are the called according to his purpose."* I kept the focus, maintained my confidence in God and I can say today, that embarking on the task is the sturdy foundation for my skill and results in the ministry. Jeremiah 29:11 *says, "For I know the thoughts that I think toward you, saith the Lord, thoughts of peace, and not of evil, to give you an expected end."*

To obey is not to be obstinate but to be yielded to God so we are not obsolete. Being in line with God's Will brings blessings while disobedience is to stray from the Father's nurturing. The blessing of the Lord makes rich and adds no sorrow (Proverbs 10:22). God will always plan blessing and no sorrows for us, for His instructions are for our good. Therefore it is wisdom to live in line with God's instruction in order for a fulfilling life.

We see that Abraham's blessing for obedience was so great that the Lord also spoke to Isaac, Abraham's son in Genesis 26:2-6 (NIV), *"The* Lord appeared to Isaac and said, "Do not go down to Egypt; live in the land where I tell you to live. 3 Stay in this land for a while, and I will be with you and will bless you. For to you and your descendants I will give all these lands and will confirm the oath I swore to your father Abraham. 4 I will make your descendants as numerous as the stars in the sky and will give them all these lands, and through your offspring all nations on earth will be blessed, 5 because Abraham obeyed me and did everything I required of him, keeping my commands, my decrees and my instructions." *6 So Isaac stayed in Gerar."*

The Word of God attests in Revelations 3:8 that God rewards obedience. We deny God's ways when we ignore His Words. If we say we are Christians and do not operate according to God's will, the Bible lets us know that God cannot be deceived. Matthew 7:21 tells us that, *"Not every one that saith unto me, Lord, Lord, shall enter into the kingdom of heaven; but he that doeth the will of my Father which is in heaven."*

Doing God's will requires outright obedience without compromising. It means not even our limitations should stop us from doing the Father's will. Full obedience does not consider what cannot be done but what God says to be done because the power to do it is derived from Him. In Philippians 4:13 Paul says, *"I can do all things through Christ which strengtheneth me."* Outright obedience does not consider circumstances but is determined to observe God's Word. Obedience considers Proverbs 23:26 which says, *"My son, give me thine heart, and let thine eyes observe my ways."* In essence, regardless of any opposing force, determined obedience complements the will of God by full submission, viewing things the way God sees them and anticipating the end result as God expects.

Obedience at times will require radical compliance with God's ways against all odds. It involves demonstration of confidence in a well-meaning and faithful God. In Jeremiah 29:11 we read that God's plans for us are plans of good and not of evil to give us the expected end. Despite Nehemiah's deprived position, God told him to approach the King to rebuild the wall of Jerusalem and amazingly, rather than a negative response from the King, Nehemiah got his favour. "... *And the king granted me, according to the good hand of my God upon me."* (Nehemiah 2:8). God backed Nehemiah up!

In some cases things might look rather difficult, making obedience really hard. In this type of situation, what we must do is keep our focus and depend on God for the required grace and strength. The Bible says He gives power to the weak and those without strength, He gives strength (Isaiah 40:29), so no matter the ordeal, we must keep relying on God knowing that His plans end ultimately in good (Jeremiah 29:11).

Since we also know that God's Word does not return to Him void (Isaiah 55:11), that He will always do what He says He will do, it is therefore wisdom to remain in His will, availing ourselves the opportunity of reward and the blessings in fulfilling His plan and purposes. It was hard for Jonah to go to Nineveh and for Gideon who deemed himself mighty to lead the war against the Midianites. Judges 6:14-16 says, *"And the Lord looked upon him, and said, Go in this thy might, and thou shalt save Israel from the hand of the Midianites: have not I sent thee? 15 And he said unto him, Oh my Lord, wherewith shall I save Israel? Behold, my family is poor in Manasseh, and I am the least in my father's house. 16 And the Lord said unto him, Surely I will be with thee, and thou shalt smite the Midianites as one man."*

Gideon found it hard. Fear was upon him but he forgot that God knew his weakness before giving the instruction and that God is Almighty, very able to equip for all situations. The fact is rather than disobey, it is better to do it afraid which is better than avoiding God's intent and ending up in trouble or in sin. Jonah should have done it afraid rather than disobey. He should have trusted God enough that He would be with him and not forsake him in the task; that God's plans for us are not evil and that Jehovah would back him up instead of him having to end up in the belly of the fish (Jonah 1:17).

When we consider instructions like showing love to our enemies, praying for those who despitefully use us (Matthew 5:44), that these are commands Jesus Christ complied with. Grace and the ability to do the extraordinary have been conferred on us as children of God. One thing we must know and not forget is that the opposing process and situations (pain, fear, humiliation, embarrassment etc) through obedience will pass, but the reward of carrying out the instruction is lasting. *"...who for the joy that was set before him endured the cross, despising the shame...."* (Hebrews 12:2).

At childbirth a woman goes through the processes of fear, pain and the pang of childbirth, an inescapable "order to be obeyed" when labour sets in. No woman is able to resist complying with this force and order of labour but to simply just comply with the process that brings the reward of a new life to birth. As soon as the baby is born, the woman in no time forgets the process (the pain and turmoil of labour) and begins to adore the outcome of her process of pain. The result, which is the bundle of joy (the baby) in her hands, far outweighs the process she underwent. In essence, we must not focus on the procedure or process but the outcome of obedience.

Obedience is dear to God's heart and He really does honour it. As our obedience honours God, as a manner of our submission to Him, God honours us in return with lasting blessings. David did not dare to touch the Lord's anointed (Saul) at the several opportunities he had to get back at Saul who was after his life. He had good reasons for self-defence but rather, David abided by God's instruction (1 Chronicles 16:22) not to touch (harm) His anointed, choosing to depend on God's protection (Psalm 23). Little wonder he won God's heart by His outright obedience, never losing any battle since he had not fought his 'battle' with Saul by himself but relied and complied with God's instruction. Little wonder also that God conferred the dynasty to his lineage (Psalm 112:1-3) with the privilege of the Royal Birth of Jesus coming from his family line (Matthew 1:6-16).

We must make up our minds to do God's will, whatever He will have us do. Let the word in Isaiah 50:7 propel and motivate us: *"For the Lord God will help me; therefore shall I not be confounded: therefore have I set my face like a flint, and I know that I shall not be ashamed."*

Surrendering to the all-knowing God, His supreme and perfect purpose truly gives an expected perfect end. Surrendering in obeying God means you consider God's rationale and reason only and not yours in every given situation. In Acts 16:6-7 the Holy Spirit instructed the apostles not to go yet to certain places. The cause of sharing the gospel is good and a great commission, a necessity for life, but because God knows best and since God's thoughts are not our thoughts (Isaiah 55:8). We see Paul demonstrate obedience to this instruction in Acts 20:16.

God's Word is God. John 1:1 says, <u>*"In the beginning was the Word*</u>, *and* <u>*the Word was*</u>

with God, and the Word was God". In essence, to respond to the Word is to respond to God. Obedience is the function of the Lordship of the Word in our lives. By allowing every Word from God to dominate our lives, guide our thoughts, decisions and actions, it enables active, steadfast and consistent obedience.

Wisdom is the principal thing; the Bible says in Proverbs 4:7. It is imperative and essential for life. God's Word gives wisdom. Hearing it, reading it and obeying it results in wisdom. As we abide in God's Word, we equip ourselves with knowledge, understanding and power to be over life's situations and circumstances. Knowing and reverencing the Lord, doing His Word and abiding in it, guides us in the path of wisdom and life. The same Word of God that enriched Solomon in wisdom and wealth says to us in Proverbs 3:6, *"In all thy ways acknowledge Him (God), and He shall direct thy paths."* Notice that The Bible did not say in some of your ways, but in all (every one) of your ways.

The fear of God is the beginning of Wisdom, the Bible says in Psalm 111:10. It means when you reverence, acknowledge and honour God with respect for His Word, giving Him first place in your life, then you are on the path of wisdom. Fear here means to revere God, His Words and His ways; the starting point for divine wisdom. The Word of God describes Daniel as having an excellent spirit all because of the fear of God in Him. He reverenced and acknowledged God in all His ways, giving respect and regard to God's Word. He honoured and submitted to God in all his ways, disregarding all opposing forces, even in the face of death. Proverbs 29:25 says, *"The fear of man bringeth a snare: but whoso putteth his trust in the Lord shall be safe."*

Indeed by trusting to do according to God's Word, Daniel was made safe and also able to proliferate the sovereignty of God (Daniel 6:25-27). He exhibited extraordinary intelligence; he was strong, able to do exploit, all because of the force of wisdom acquired by acknowledging and obeying God was active in Him.

As God's obedient children, recreated and peculiar, special, as the Bible describes us in (1 Peter 1:14 and 1 Peter 2:9), let us therefore not fail nor shirk in the service of obedience in honour of our God and Father. God told Eli in 1 Samuel 2:30 (NIV), "*....Those who honour me I will honour, but those who despise me will be disdained.*" The promises and blessings of God are for those who do what He has asked them to do. Those who hearken to His Word and voice are committed to Him and He is also faithful to them. They walk in God's will, they do not fall prey to sin. Galatians 5:16 says, "*This I say then, walk in the Spirit, and ye shall not fulfil the lust of the flesh.*"

Living in the fear (obedience) of God implies life (Proverbs 19:23 NIV). This therefore means disobedience to God implies death due to being severed. Leviticus 18:4-5(CEV) says, "*I am the Lord your God, and you must obey my teachings. Obey them and you will live. I am the Lord.*" In Romans 8:6 the Bible states, "*For to be carnally minded is death; but to be spiritually minded is life and peace.*" The Bible's says blessed are you when you suffer for righteousness (1 Peter 3:14). It is safer to undergo and tolerate the demands of obedience than to suffer for the sin of disobedience. As we demonstrate our trust in God through obedience, God gives us the blessings accrued through obedience. Attaining these rewards and blessings further stimulates our trust in God. By so doing, we are building a relationship of trust.

As God's children, who rely and depend on Him and would also truly heed His Word, in situation like Paul's in Acts 16:6-7, we must render full compliance without misgivings. True submission to God requires absolute obedience. As we see in Matthew 18:3-4, *"And said, Verily I say unto you, Except ye be converted, and become as little children, ye shall not enter into the kingdom of heaven. 4 Whosoever therefore shall humble himself as this little child, the same is greatest in the kingdom of heaven."*

Training ourselves in obedience is vital; it advances our walk with God from one level to another as we receive and obey His directions from His written Word and spoken Words (to our spirits). David relied on God's Word; obeying and relying on It in order to live a perfect life. 2 Samuel 22:33 says, *"God is my strength and power: and he makes my way perfect."*

We are to delight in God's Word for a great life like the Psalmist who passionately and zealously obeyed God, and remained in His will. (See Psalm 119:14-20, 24, 30-36,44-45,47-48, 97-100,130 NIV). We must stay determined to walk in obedience, never compromising obeying God but being resolute like the Psalmist. Our obedience is indicative of our level of submission to God. It is for our own good that we constantly heighten our level of submission to God. Proverbs 4:22 says His Word is life to those who find (submit to and do) them.

Not fully doing as The Lord requires is disobedience. This is because if it is not absolute obedience it isn't obedience at all. In 1 John 3:4 the Bible says sin is the transgression of the Law (The instructions, precepts, will and the commands of God). The Israelites did not completely drive out the inhabitants of Canaan as instructed by the all-knowing and supreme God; this led to compromise in intermarriage with the initial inhabitants and the worshiping of their idols.

By walking against God's will, disobeying His instruction they sinned against God.

The Bible records in Numbers 33:55-56 the profound warning given them *"But if ye will not drive out the inhabitants of the land from before you; then it shall come to pass, that those which ye let remain of them shall be pricks in your eyes, and thorns in your sides, and shall vex you in the land wherein ye dwell. 56 Moreover it shall come to pass, that I shall do unto you, as I thought to do unto them."*

Saul also in 1 Samuel 15 did not completely destroy the Amalekites as instructed. This meant sin, and Samuel had to bring The Lord's rebuke to the King (Saul). As verse 22-23 shows, *"And Samuel said, Hath the Lord as great delight in burnt offerings and sacrifices, as in obeying the voice of the Lord? Behold, to obey is better than sacrifice, and to hearken than the fat of rams. 23 For rebellion is as the sin of witchcraft, and stubbornness is as iniquity and idolatry. Because thou hast rejected the word of the Lord, he hath also rejected thee from being king."*

Our obedience pleases and honours God, who in turn blesses us. Psalm 35:27 says, *"Let them shout for joy, and be glad, that favour my righteous cause: yea, let them say continually, Let the LORD be magnified, which hath pleasure in the prosperity of his servant.*"

Abraham portrayed trust and confidence in God Who is all-able. He satisfied God by his obedience which was irrespective of all prevailing circumstance. He obeyed God steadfastly to the point of giving up his son Isaac. He did not put anything in life above the will of God his Maker. Absolutely nothing was of more importance to him than what God would have him do.

Galatians 5:16 says, "Walk *in the Spirit* (God and His ways) *and ye shall not fulfil the lust of the flesh* (the cares of the world)."

Abraham prevailed in obedience, qualifying as one God could call a friend. In all his ways, he acknowledged the supremacy of his Maker, relying on the safety that is sure in the sovereign God.

Proverbs 1:33 records God's saying, *"But whoso hearkeneth unto Me shall dwell in safety, and shall be quiet from fear of evil."* Abraham submitted his will to the will of God so as not to submit to the lust of the flesh. He recognised God as Jehovah-Shammah, (The Lord is There); there for him in all situations, trustworthy and dependable, true to His words and all-able in all circumstances. He trusted God with all his heart, not allowing circumstances or his condition to dictate to him.

Our responsiveness to God is also a demonstration of our love for Him. As we delight in His will, our spirits respond in obedience, a proof of our love. 1 John 5:2-3 (NIV) says, *"This is how we know that we love the children of God: by loving God and carrying out his commands. 3 In fact, this is love for God: to keep his commands. And his commands are not burdensome"*. In John 14:15 also, the Bible says, *"If you love me, keep my commandments."* To say Jesus is Lord over our lives is to say we surrender all to His Lordship, implying trust in Him in all situations. This therefore means that obeying Him should not be a struggle. Obedience signifies loyalty and stewardship. It is power and life to those that live by it (Proverbs 4:10). Obeying God channels your life and your plans in His direction. The Bible says God's plans for us are plans of good and not of evil to give a hope and a future (Jeremiah 29:11 NIV). A truly obedient life is fully surrendered to all of God's Word.

1 Samuel 15 has an account of disobedience and its devastating effect as seen in the life of Saul who did not fully comply with God's instruction. Prophet Samuel stressed to him in verse 22 that, "....*to obey is better than sacrifice, and to hearken than the fat of rams. 23. For rebellion is a sin of witchcraft and stubbornness is as iniquity and idolatry, because thou hast rejected the word of the Lord, He hath also rejected thee from being king.*" In 1 Samuel 15:24 (NIV) it says, "*Then Saul said to Samuel, I have sinned. I violated the Lord's command and your instructions. I was afraid of the men and so I gave in to them.*"

He disobeyed God and sinned because he feared the people and obeyed their voice. What a choice!

From the last scripture, we see that disobedience is to rebel, it is arrogance and pride. The implications of such sin can be costly and its effect permanent.

Those not being submissive to God are referred to in Psalm 107:10-12.

Saul lost the dynasty from His generation for a seemly good excuse of offering God a sacrifice. 1 Samuel 15:21(NIV) says, *"The soldiers took sheep and cattle from the plunder, the best of what was devoted to God, in order to sacrifice them to the Lord your God at Gilgal."* Couldn't Saul have instructed his soldiers to destroy them all? What a lame excuse; He forgot that God owns all things, he does not have to possess them for God and if God is to be impressed, it is only by doing His command. But he lost the throne through disobedience to David, who was settled on obedience. He said in Psalm 40:6-8, *"Sacrifice and offering thou didst not desire; mine ears hast thou opened: burnt offering and sin offering hast thou not required.7 Then said I, Lo, I come: in the volume of the book it is written of me,8 I delight to do thy will, O my God: yea, thy law is within my heart."*

Nevertheless God's Word still came to David in Psalm 132:12, *"If thy children keep my covenant* and *my testimonies that I shall teach them, their children shall also sit upon thy throne for evermore."*

When we compare Abraham's reaction to God's Word and the result he got with Saul's, it is indicative that we as God's creations ought to heed the will of our Creator over our own will or that of any of other God's creation. To do the will of men is a misdeed and it is to sin (Proverbs 29:25). Hear the words of a determined man; following God's instruction in Mark 16:15-16 for us all to reach out and share the Good News (Gospel) to the world. Paul said in 1 Corinthians 9:16-17, *"For though I preach the gospel, I have nothing to glory of: for necessity is laid upon me; yea, woe is unto me, if I preach not the gospel! 17 For if I do this thing willingly, I have a reward: but if against my will, a dispensation of the gospel is committed unto me."* This simply portrays Paul as self-motivated in the cause of obedience.

In John 14:6 Jesus says He is the way, the truth and life. Therefore we will not be lost as we allow Him to guide and direct us into the blessing that follows obeying Him.

By keeping in line, in form and in tune with God, our cares are taken care of. The Bible says in Jeremiah 17:7, *"Blessed is the man that trusts in the Lord, and whose hope the Lord is"*. By seeking to do the will of God first, our cares are taken care of as we abide in God through obedience to His Word. Matthew 6:33 says, *"But seek ye first the kingdom of God, and his righteousness; and all these things shall be added unto you."*

Joshua, the leader of Israelites' armed forces was obedient to a seemingly ridiculous instruction that, to bring down the huge wall of Jericho, they are to simply have the people march around the wall, blow the trumpet, shout and praise God. The Bible says in Hebrews 11:30 that 'by faith (their obedient action), the walls of Jericho fell down.

Obedience characterises our faith in God and His Word. It typifies our faith in Him. Mary the mother of Jesus said to the servants in John 2:5, *"Whatsoever he saith unto you, do it"*. Just like Abraham, we see his son

Isaac's obedience in Genesis 26:2-6, *"And the Lord appeared unto him, and said, Go not down into Egypt; dwell in the land which I shall tell thee of: 3 Sojourn in this land, and I will be with thee, and will bless thee; for unto thee, and unto thy seed, I will give all these countries, and I will perform the oath which I sware unto Abraham thy father;4 And I will make thy seed to multiply as the stars of heaven, and will give unto thy seed all these countries; and in thy seed shall all the nations of the earth be blessed;5 Because that Abraham obeyed my voice, and kept my charge, my commandments, my statutes, and my laws.6 And Isaac dwelt in Gerar."* In verses 13-14 we see the result of his obedience, *"And the man waxed great, and went forward, and grew until he became very great: 14 For he had possession of flocks, and possession of herds, and great store of servants: and the Philistines envied him."*

As followers of Jesus our lives must depict dedicated obedience, not only in proclaiming Him as Master, Lord and Saviour but also by being in full compliance with His will in absolute terms. As we see in Matthew 17:1-5 *"And after six days Jesus taketh Peter, James,* *and John his brother, and bringeth them up into an high mountain apart,2 And was transfigured before them: and his face did shine as the sun, and his raiment was white as the light.3 And, behold, there appeared unto them Moses and Elias talking with him.4 Then answered Peter, and said unto Jesus, Lord, it is good for us to be here: if thou wilt, let us make here three tabernacles; one for thee, and one for Moses, and one for Elias. 5 While he yet spake, **behold, a bright cloud overshadowed them: and behold a voice out of the cloud, which said, This is my beloved Son, in whom I am well pleased; <u>hear ye him</u>.*** " This profound instruction in Matthew 17:5 was given to Jesus' disciples while on the mount of transfiguration for them not just to follow Jesus <u>but essentially to obey Him</u>.

Obedience affirms our faith in God while disobedience implies our doubts. The Word of God gives us many essential instructions for life as followers of Christ. Jesus instructed His disciples (us) in Mark 16:15, *"Go ye into all the world, and preach the gospel to every creature."* -A specific instruction to all of us His followers to reach out and share the Good

News to the world. Confidence and trust in God propels our obedience and is bound to be backed by the power of the Holy Spirit, our Enabler who will help us. John 15:26 (Amp) says, *"But when the Comforter (Counsellor, Helper, Advocate, Intercessor, Strengthener, Standby) comes, Whom I will send to you from the Father, the Spirit of Truth Who comes (proceeds) from the Father, He [Himself] will testify regarding Me."*

As we depend on God through the power of the Holy Spirit through any daunting act of obedience, He is with you (John 14:18), in you (1 John 4:4), and He is by you to teach (John 14:26), lead and guide you (Proverbs 3:5-6) unto accomplishment and victory. As we abide in God's Word, we make progress, hence we are transformed from one level of glory to another (2 Corinthians 3:18).

The key to a fulfilling life is ardent obedience. Wisdom, peace, joy and many other blessings are products of our fellowship with God and our love for Him through obedience (2 John 1:6). These are the Words of Jesus Christ in Luke 6:46-49, *"And why call ye me, Lord, Lord, and do not the things which I say? 47*

Whosoever cometh to me, and heareth my sayings, and doeth them, I will shew you to whom he is like:48 He is like a man which built an house, and digged deep, and laid the foundation on a rock: and when the flood arose, the stream beat vehemently upon that house, and could not shake it: for it was founded upon a rock.49 But he that heareth, and doeth not, is like a man that without a foundation built an house upon the earth; against which the stream did beat vehemently, and immediately it fell; and the ruin of that house was great."

In John 14:15 Jesus said, *"If you love me, keep my commandments."*

In John 15:10 he said, *"If ye keep my commandments, ye shall abide in my love; even as I have kept my Father's commandments, and abide in his love."*

In John 15:14 Jesus said, *"You are my friends, if you do whatsoever I command you."*

James 1:22 admonishes us to be doers of the Word of God and not just hearers so we are not deceiving our own ourselves. The one who does not obey God disobeys simply because he does not have enough faith in God to trust, rely and depend on His Words enough to act on it. Revelations 2:29 says that he who has ears, let him hear. Doers hear to do the Word, doing themselves the good derived from acting on God's instructions which the Bible say are not grievous (1 John 5:3).

The blessings of obedience are great. This is because as we honour God by it, God in return honours and reward our actions. It is imperative that we discern the will and plans of God, effectively acting upon them as obedient children perfectly in sync with the Father.

Acting upon God's Word by yielding and adhering to it is wisdom. Psalm 119:9 (NCV) says, *"How can a young person live a pure life? By obeying your word."* Psalm 19:7-8 (NCV) says, *"The teachings of the Lord are perfect; they give new strength. The rules of the Lord can be trusted; they make plain people wise. 8 The orders of the Lord are right; they make people happy. The commands of the Lord are pure; they light up the way.* "Paul said to the elders from Ephesus in Acts 20:32 (NCV),

"Now I am putting you in the care of God and the message about his grace. It is able to give you strength, and it will give you the blessings God has for all his holy people."

The Word of God is for doing that it may promote us in life. Proverbs 10:17 says, *"He is in the way of life that keepeth instruction: but he that refuseth reproof erreth."* Delay or not fully complying with; as well as total refusal in doing God's will means to disobey which implies rebellion. If we say we are God's and truly believe, then we must fully obey. That is the reason why Jesus in Hebrews 5:9 is described as "the author of eternal salvation to all who obey Him".

Psalms 95:7-8 *says,* "For he is our God; and we are the people of his pasture, and the sheep of his hand. Today if ye will hear his voice, *8. Harden not your heart, as in the provocation, and as in the day of temptation in the wilderness."* Faith is useless without works (action, obedience) as we see in James 2:17, 26 so no matter what, as obedient children, God's Word must be acted upon. Acting on God's Word, brings confidence of His security and His backing, being at peace

(Isaiah 26:3) because you are doing what you are supposed to do and hence where you are supposed to be – in the perfect plan of God. By this, you dwell in the light and not in darkness (of God's Word and will). Remember John calls Him the True Light (John 1:9).

The Bible records Jesus saying in John 5:30 (Amp), *"I am able to do nothing from Myself [independently, of My own accord— but only as I am taught by God and as I get His orders]. Even as I hear, I judge [I decide as I am bidden to decide. As the voice comes to Me, so I give a decision], and My judgment is right (just, righteous), because I do not seek* or consult My own will [I have no desire to do what is pleasing to Myself, My own aim, My own purpose] but only the will and pleasure of the Father Who sent Me."

Just as Jesus, God's expectation of us also is to correspond to His will in order for great accomplishment. In Mark 4:39-41 we see the wind and sea obey Jesus, the fig tree also (Mark 11:13-14, 21) even the dead (John 11:43-44), all obeyed Him because He walked in line, in form and in tune with the Father.

**"When we obey God, we are
sure that we know him."
1 John 2:3 (CEV)**

A song in confession of obedience

I'll say yes, oh yes!
To Your will and to Your way
I'll say yes, oh yes!
I will trust you and obey
When Your Spirit speaks to me
With my whole heart I'll agree,
And my answer will be yes, oh yes!

Chapter 2

In Time

"I made haste, and delayed not to keep
thy commandments".
Psalm119:60

Obedience to God requires timely action.
To delay is to deny the purpose as delay
compromises the goal. Carrying out
God's Word to precision honours God. His
instruction must be at His time and not ours,
not when it is convenient for us but as God
wants it done in order that we may achieve
God's purpose. Obedience is at God's time
and not man's time. Procrastinating God's
Word is disobedience.

Abraham did not delay or hesitate in the
instruction to sacrifice Isaac. He did what
God said to do at the particular time
fulfilling the particular purpose or goal

for a blessing (Genesis 22:1-18). Abraham was focused in strict compliance with God's directives. He was determined and punctual. *"And Abraham <u>rose up early</u> in the morning."* (Genesis 22:3). Viewing God's instruction as paramount, he did not hesitate in complying with The Owner and Maker of all things, the Provider and Giver of Isaac. Abraham's trust and confidence in God is portrayed by His timely and determined response.

Genesis 22:7-8 says, *"And Isaac spake unto Abraham his father, and said, 'My father' and he said, 'Here am I, my son'. And he said, 'Behold the fire and the wood: but where is the lamb for a burnt offering?' And Abraham said, 'My son, **God will provide** himself a lamb for a burnt offering': so they went both of them together."*

In Romans 4:20-22 it says, *"He staggered not at the promise of God through unbelief; but was strong in faith, giving glory to God; **And being fully persuaded that, what he had promised, he was able also to perform**. And therefore it was imputed to him for righteousness."* Indeed our timely response to God's instruction is characteristic of our confidence in Him.

As God's children having been redeemed, with a new nature, the nature of the Father; the Bible states in Romans 6:14 that sin (amongst which is disobedience) should no longer have dominion over us. Hence we make conscious effort to rule over any sinful nature to delay and deny the flow of God's will through us; by enforcing that we respond instantly to the Words of our Heavenly Father. In John 4:34, *"Jesus saith unto them, My meat is to do the will of him that sent me, and to finish his work."* In doing God's will, we must be resolute, timely and exact like Jesus in doing the Father's will, not permitting any delay or hindrances.

The Bible records of Noah in Hebrews 11:7-8 (TLB) that, *"Noah was another who trusted God. When he heard God's warning about the future, Noah believed Him even though there was then no sign of flood, and **wasting no time**, he built the ark and saved his family. Noah's belief in God was in direct contrast to the sin and disbelief of the rest of the world — which refused to obey-and because of his* *faith he became one of those whom God has accepted. 8. Abraham trusted God, and when God told him to leave home and go far away to another land which He promised to give him, **Abraham obeyed. Away he went**, not even knowing where he was going."* By their prompt and loyal action, we see men with obedient hearts, men of action to God's instruction, men who were timely and effective in their response to God's Word.

Obedience entails complying with and not opposing God's will, thus fulfilling His ultimate purpose. To walk in obedience is to abide in God's will. We see Moses in Exodus 4:10-17 in a dialogue with God over his limitations, doubts, and apprehension. All were overcome by Moses trusting God amid his fears, speedily launching into obedience — not entertaining delay or dissuasion — but immediately doing as God instructed. As Exodus 4:18 says, *"And Moses went and returned to Jethro his father in law, and said unto him, Let me go, I pray thee, and return unto my brethren which are in Egypt, and see whether they be yet alive. And Jethro said to Moses, Go in peace."* It is the obedience done to time and with precision that moves God.

Obedience to God must be the absolute (Deuteronomy 12:32). To say we revere God means to do His complete will. Deuteronomy 8:6 (NIV) says, *"Observe the commands of the Lord your God, walking in obedience to him and revering him."* God recognises full obedience as we see in the life of Abraham. The Bible states that those who observe lying vanities forsake their own mercy (Jonah 2:8). Therefore we must not allow anything hinder us nor take the place of God in us, for He must always have the first and final say. Anything that takes priority in our lives takes the place of God in our lives and becomes our god and the Bible clearly states in Exodus 34:14 (CEV) that, *"I demand your complete loyalty — you must not worship any other god!"*

I remember receiving divine inspiration and instruction to write Christian books in 2009. Writing was not anything I'd ever considered doing, but I remember many years back that a prophecy was given that I would write.

I had no interest in writing at all but when the instruction came I knew clearly inside me that my not complying regardless of all my 'good reasons' would mean disobeying the Spirit of God and failing God. I considered my loving relationship with God and knew I could not defy Him. I certainly did not want any regret and recognised the fact that I serve a God whose plans for me should supersede mine.

Considering all these things, I jolted myself to action (remembering Colossians 4:17 which says, *"Take heed to the ministry which thou hast received in the Lord, that thou fulfil it."*) and I settled it in my heart that I had NO CHOICE but to start to write.

I began to write and God was with me every step of the way, supplying divine help and inspiration. I finished the first book and amazed myself when, at the end of 2009, I had produced two books. Since then, I have written a book each year by God's grace. According to His Word in Psalm 138:8, *"The Lord will perfect that which concerneth me: thy mercy, O Lord, endureth for ever: forsake not the works of thine own hands."*

God has kept these words at the forefront of each writing assignment and interestingly today, I can now say that I love and enjoy writing. It is one of the things I do now, a part of me which obedience allowed God to develop in me, proving God's word in Luke 1:37 that nothing is impossible with God. His Word also says in Isaiah 55:6, *"Seek ye the Lord while he may be found, call ye upon him (act in response) while he is near:"* When we act at God's Word, we access God's result for timely move.

Be quick to obey — the response and action required by you may be tied to a timed blessing for you or linked to someone you know. We might not know the intention, so we must be prompt in reaction, carrying out God's plan for the fulfillment of His purpose, both known and unknown to us. There are situations where we could be God's agent at a particular time for a prayer to be answered. Someone could just have been praying and God wants to use us as the means to answering the prayers. Therefore, never resist God as it is a privilege to be His means, His reliable and dependable driving force. Proverbs 3:27 says, *"Withhold not good from them to whom it is due, when it is in the power of thine hand to do it."* God blessed us that we may also be a blessing to others. Genesis 12:2 too says, *"...thou shalt be a blessing,"* His tool of blessing to others. Our timely response saves lives and situations. Reluctance, delay and doubting God's Word are acts of disobedience which destroy and end in regret.

The Bible says in James 2:26 that faith without works is dead, being alone just as the body without the spirit is dead. Therefore our faith in God must work hand-in-hand with our immediate action to His directives; meaning we believe and action it. In Romans 10:17 we read that, *"faith comes by hearing, and hearing by the Word of God".* As we are exposed to God's Word, faith (for action) comes to us.

If we really have the faith that God's Word is infallible, that His Word has efficacy, then we must have the corresponding faith to put His Words to action without doubts or hesitation. When we do not stagger through unbelief irrespective of circumstance just like Abraham (Romans 4:20), we are said to also have pleased God. This demonstration of confidence in God qualifies us for greater glories. Abraham's faith and obedience qualified him to be called by God His friend (James 2:23).

Inactive faith will die because it is independent of action. We see this in James 2:17, *"Even so faith, if it hath not works, is dead, being alone."* So when faith has no action due to inaction (disobedience), it dies as a result of us being hearers only and not doers of the Word. As James 1:22 (The Message translation) advises, *"Don't fool yourself into thinking that you are a listener when you are anything but, letting the Word go in one ear and out the other. <u>Act on what you hear!</u>"*

The Psalmist says in Psalm 119:105, *"Thy word is a lamp unto my feet, and a light unto my path."* Focus on dwelling on His Word and living it. Jesus gave these words in John 16:13, *"Howbeit when he, the Spirit of truth, is come, he will guide you into all truth: for he shall not speak of himself; but whatsoever he shall hear, that shall he speak: and he will show you things to come";* promising us supernatural guidance and constancy of support as we journey through life.

Full and complete obedience entails being prompt in action. Full obedience means doing what is required at His time and as told. The Bible says in Philippians 2:13, *"For it is God which worketh in you both to will and to do of his good pleasure."*

In Acts 8:29-30,*"Then the Spirit said unto Philip, Go near, and join thyself to this chariot.30 <u>And Philip ran thither to him,</u> and heard him read the prophet Esaias, and said, Understandest thou what thou readest?"* The Bible points out in verse 30 that He did it quickly with urgency. We see that Philip ran to action, immediately effecting the instruction received by the Spirit of God, just as he was told.

Obedience involves absolute compliance. God detests procrastinating, not being reactive to His command. When God gives instructions, He requires timely corresponding action. To delay is to disobey. To react at our own time and not His, is dishonour. When you respond to God, you can be confident for His response too.

Every Word of God that we put to action works for our good (Romans 8:28). As we keep obedience to God's Word and instruction as priority, we keep well and triumphant through life. Joshua 1:8 says, *"This book of the law shall not depart out of thy mouth; but thou shalt meditate therein day and night, that thou mayest observe to do according to all that is written therein: for then thou shalt make thy way prosperous, and then thou shalt have good success."* Each result that our obedient action produces further stimulates and conditions our spirits for greater results of obedience. Proverbs 16:20 (New Revised Standard Version) says that *"Those who are attentive to a matter will prosper and happy are those who trust in the Lord."*

We read in the Bible that Deborah the prophetess responded, not procrastinating and waiting for another occasion to accompany Barak to battle. The Shunammite woman reacted promptly to Elisha's need of accommodation which resulted in recompense for her; a gift of a child she never had.

Simon Peter and Andrew obeyed; following the Master straightaway. Matthew 4:20 says, *"And they straightway left their nets, and followed him."*

Esther reacted immediately to the dilemma of the Jews without delay. Our promptness preserves, saves and improves, directly or indirectly, situations or circumstances that we are either aware or unaware of.

We see in Genesis 17:11-23 how Abraham took God's order wholeheartedly with a submissive heart and attitude, complying and conforming in accordance to God's instruction. In the same vein, God expects of us also to obey at the first instance, first-hand, obeying completely and fully in all circumstances, convenient or not, fully submitted, assured that His plans for us are good (Jeremiah 29:11).

The following scriptures illustrates how when we obey entirely, God shows up by His corresponding actions.

In temptations, God is ever so faithful, providing a way of escape (1 Corinthians 10:13), He makes a way where there seems to be no way (Isaiah 43:19), it works together for our good (Romans 8:28).

- Abraham got the ram to kill instead of Isaac (Genesis 22:1-18).
- Daniel was untouched in the lion's den. (Daniel 6:16-24).
- The three Hebrew boys were unscathed by fire (Daniel 3:14-30).
- Divine supplies and restoration came for the widow of Zarephath (1 Kings 17).

They all obeyed putting into action God's word, resilient in trust, despite their situations and regardless of the implication of the instruction received. Their various actions glorified God and in turn, God glorified Himself in them; rewarding each of them for their obedience. We must therefore also ensure that our own obedience is carried out with precision, in time and in sync with God's perfect plan.

True submission and the love of the Lord makes you correspond in active obedience. Deuteronomy 6:5 says, *"And thou shalt love the Lord thy God with all thine heart, and with all thy soul, and with all thy might."* When we allow the love and fear (reverence in respect and honour) of God to consume and rule our minds, we will not struggle to comply with His will.

At certain times, instruction may be daunting and may not add up with our situation, for example the widow of Zarephath who gave up all she and her son had for Elijah. However her response was timely for a blessing from the man of God, Elijah. Obedience is stimulated by reverence for God. Timely reaction is born out of love and honour of the Father. John 14:16 (TLB) says, *"If you love Me, obey Me."* It connotes responsiveness that His will be done through us. Also, as we give heed to the Word of God at God's time, God's way and not ours, we align with divine purpose.

Obedience boosts our knowledge of God and enhances our walk with Him. Obedience empowers. It is the very first step towards answers to prayers as strength can be derived from it. (2 Samuel 22:33)

Jesus' obedience even unto death typifies His perfection (Hebrews 5:9). He was completely obedient unto God, even to civil instructions of authority during His days on earth, He was obedient. His disciple, Peter followed suit, he obeyed not doubting instruction to get money from the fish's mouth but trusting the Master. He did not doubt, argue or fuss over

Jesus' instruction. Neither did Jesus disobey the authority of the land too by not fulfilling civil obligations (Matthew 17:24-27). In verse 27, we see that Peter's obedience paid him off as his bill was also settled: "...*that take, and give unto them for me and thee.*"

Noah received specification on timing, measurement and design for building the ark. The earth was being filled with violence; God revealed to Noah that there was going to be a great flood which would destroy man from the face of the earth. God found Noah reliable in righteousness and obedience which qualified him as dependable to handle the peculiar task of building an ark for preserving the lives of his family and some animals.

However Jonah, called to go as a missionary to Nineveh, was reluctant to follow God's instruction, and did not act in time. He had too much concern for his own reputation, and did not avail himself of God's divine outcome for a set time which he ended up regretting. He eventually complied after his ordeal in the belly of a whale but what an opportunity it would have been for him to be an effective part of God's plan at the very first instance? We see that fear tormented him out of a perfect divine plan and the blessing of instantaneous obedience. If we say we trust and love God, then we must obey Him instantaneously without fear. As it says in 1 John 4:18, *"There is no fear in love; but perfect love casteth out fear: because fear hath torment. He that feareth is not made perfect in love."*

Fear must not hinder our service of honour in obedience to God. Disobedience means to dishonour, reject, ignore, avoid, or to discount the good plan of God for us (Jeremiah 29:11). The consequences of disobedience can be very costly hence we must obey God absolutely. The word of God is wisdom. Proverbs 4:5 *says, "Get wisdom, get understanding: forget it not; neither decline from the words of My mouth."* Any word from God brings wisdom and understanding; the enlightenment required for the victorious life (Psalm 119:130). In our lives therefore, no Word of God is to be declined.

1 Peter 1:14 says, *"As obedient children, not fashioning yourselves according to the former*

lusts in your ignorance." The Scripture regard us as obedient therefore we must walk in the light of how the Word of God sees us. It means with determination we can respond promptly to God and His Word. Isaiah describes his obedience and determination as well as simultaneous confidence in God in Isaiah 50:5-7(NIV). He says, *"The Sovereign Lord has opened my ears; I have not been rebellious, I have not turned away.6 I offered my back to those who beat me, my cheeks to those who pulled out my beard; did not hide my face* from *mocking and spitting 7 Because the Sovereign Lord helps me, I will not be disgraced. Therefore have I set my face like flint, and I know I will not be put to shame."*

As obedient children, we are expected to be open to his instructions just like Abraham while living with His Father in Haran received a message from the Lord calling upon him to separate himself from the old associations and go to Canaan. He obeyed the call and he became blessed. Obedience avails us of God's favour meaning our actions generate God's reaction.

When we receive divine instruction, through the Holy Spirit our Helper, He will guide us into all truth. John 16:13 says, *"Howbeit when he, the Spirit of truth, is come, he will guide you into all truth: for he shall not speak of himself; but whatsoever he shall hear, that shall he speak: and he will show you things to come."* God also grants the ability through the same Holy Spirit Who promises to be with us through the commission given us. (Matthew 28:18-20). The Holy Spirit as our Teacher, Helper and Standby is a guarantee for support through the journey of obedience. John 14:26 (Amplified Bible) says, *"But the Comforter (Counsellor, Helper, Intercessor, Advocate, Strengthener, Standby), the Holy Spirit, Whom the Father will send in My name [in My place, to represent Me and act on My behalf], He will teach you all things. And He will cause you to recall (will remind you of, bring to your remembrance) everything I have told you."* God will not abandon us through it (Hebrews 13:5), He will be with us, all we need to do is just to yield and comply by faith with His Word.

The question to ask ourselves is when the Holy Spirit teaches and instructs us, will we obey? When He reminds and prompts you, will you listen and obey? To ignore the instruction, the will and guidance of the Holy Spirit is to disobey.

Galatians 5:16-19 (TLB) says, *"I advise you to obey only the Holy Spirit's instructions. He will tell you where to go and what to do, and then you won't always be doing wrong things of your evil nature wants to do. 17. For we naturally love to do evil things that are just opposite from the things that the Holy Spirit tells us to do; and the good things we want to do when the spirit has his way with us are just the opposite of our natural desires. These two forces within us are constantly fighting each other to win control over us, and our wishes are never free from their pressures. 18. When you are guided by the Holy Spirit you need no longer force yourselves to obey.... 19.But when you follow your own wrong inclination your lives will produce these evil desires...."* It is therefore imperative that in our journey of obedience that we pray for the grace to always do the will of the Father. Jesus in Luke 22:42 did this even in the face of death. He prayed, *"Not my will, but Thy will be done."* We see Jesus resolute in obedience, ensuring that the perfect will of God is done.

Matthew 26:36-42 gives an account of how Jesus engaged in prayer to draw strength in order to comply with what was ahead of Him:

*"Then cometh Jesus with them unto a hill called Gethsemane, and saith unto the disciples, sit ye here, while I go and pray yonder. 37. And He took with Him Peter and the two sons of Zebedee and begun to be sorrowful and very heavy. 38. Then saith He unto them 'My soul is exceedingly sorrowful, even unto death: tarry here, and watch with me. 39. And He went a little farther, and fell on His face, and prayed, saying 'O my Father, if it is possible, let this cup pass from me: nevertheless, **not as I will, but as Thou wilt**. 40. And He cometh unto His disciples, and findeth them asleep, and saith unto Peter, 'What, could ye not watch with Me one hour.' 41. 'Watch and pray, that ye enter not into temptation: **the spirit is indeed willing,** but the flesh is weak. 42. He went again the second time, and prayed saying, 'O my Father, if this cup (of this hard/ tough instruction) may not pass away from*

me, except I drink (I do it/carry it out), **Thy will be done.**"

We see true determination and the willingness of Jesus to obey and carry out the Father's will in verse 41 and 42. Although tough to bear, He finds strength through prayers and therefore was able to comply in obedience. He recognises that the will of the Father and the need to observe them. We see Jesus persist in prayer through determination so as to prevail over disobedience. Prayer will align and fine-tune us in God's purpose. From it we can draw strength and boldness that we require for the task. In respect for divine timing Jesus acknowledged that the time for Him to be betrayed had come and mentioned it to His disciples at Passover as an act that must be done; thus He willingly submitted to those who came for His arrest. (Matthew 26:18-19, 50-57).

The Bible says if you faint in the time of adversity your strength is small (Proverbs 24:10). The reason we need to brace ourselves in prayer is to be able to obey and do the will of God, regardless of the opposing force. Since the Word of God is perfect and we cannot improve on it, therefore we should just act upon it avoiding the sway of disobedience. Psalms 19:7-8 says, *"The law of the Lord is perfect, converting the soul: the testimony of the Lord is sure, making wise the simple.8 The statutes of the Lord are right, rejoicing the heart: the commandment of the Lord is pure, enlightening the eyes."*

Delay in acting disqualifies, rescinds or invalidates because instruction or activity has not been carried out or observed to pre-arranged time or pre-designed. Disobedience forfeits the original purpose and it is same for partial obedience. In other words, to partly obey is to disobey. If it is not done to precision, it cannot be referred to as obedience. Erring in whatever way implies disobedience. Therefore be quick to hear and to act on God's Word received either through your spirit or from His written Word. Proverbs 30:5 says, *"Every word of God is pure: he is a shield unto them that put their trust in him."* Being prompt to do the will of God is a demonstration of confidence, trust and faith in God. God acknowledges obedience as a product of faith in Him. 1 Kings 14:8 says,*"... my servant David, who kept my commandments, and who followed me with all his heart, to do that only which was right in mine eyes."*

Obeying God must not be haphazardly but wholeheartedly. It must be done promptly and precisely without compromising God's instruction; for God cannot be deceived. Galatians 6:7 says, *"Be not deceived; God is not mocked: for whatsoever a man sows, that shall he also reap."* He sees our heart and knows our motives. The honour of the supremacy of God and fear in reverence of Him compelled Abimelech to act immediately, averting dire consequences. (Genesis 20:1-18). He reverted on his action expressly and speedily with remorse in avoidance of action that is against God's will.

Fear or the complexity involved in carrying out any particular act of obedience should never deter us where obeying God is concerned. This is in order to prevent any deterrent to our blessing. Abraham received the challenging instruction regarding circumcision and he conformed to God's will (See Genesis 17:11-27 NIV). Notice in verse 23-27 that Abraham acted promptly. *"**On that very day** Abraham* took his son Ishmael and all those born in his household or bought with his money, every male in his household, and circumcised them, as God told him. 24 Abraham was ninety-nine years old when he was circumcised 25 and his son Ishmael was thirteen; 26 Abraham and his son Ishmael were both circumcised **on that very day**. 27 And every male in Abraham's household, including those born in his household or bought from a foreigner, was circumcised with him."

When God gives His Word, by the reason of His supremacy, our action must immediately respond. In Genesis 1:3 even the earth responded immediately when God said "Let there be light" and the Bible records that "and there was light". This was same for all His other inanimate creations; they all corresponded with His Word instantaneously.

Genesis 1: 3-15 says, *"And God said, Let there be light: and there was light.4 And God saw the light, that it was good: and God divided the light from the darkness.5 And God called the light Day, and the darkness he called Night. And the evening and the morning were the first day.6 And God said, Let there be a firmament in the midst of the waters, and let it divide the waters from the waters.7 And God made the firmament, and divided the waters which were under the firmament from the waters which were above the firmament: and it was so.8 And God called the firmament Heaven. And the evening and the morning were the second day.9 And God said, Let the waters under the heaven be gathered together unto one place, and let the dry land appear:* **and it was so.***10 And God called the dry land Earth; and the gathering together of the waters called the Seas: and God saw that it was good.11 And God said, Let the earth bring forth grass, the herb yielding seed, and the fruit tree yielding fruit after his kind, whose seed is in itself, upon the earth:* **and it was so.***12 And the earth brought forth grass, and herb yielding seed after his kind, and the tree yielding fruit, whose seed was in itself, after his kind: and God saw that it was good.13 And the evening and the morning were the third day.14 And God said, Let there be lights in the firmament of the heaven to divide the day from the night; and let them be for signs, and for seasons, and for days, and years:15 And let them be for lights in the firmament of* *the heaven to give light upon the earth:* **and it was so**.*"*

Therefore as God's animate creation, made in His own image, carefully created and designed,(Psalms 139:14) we, as a sign of our superiority over all other of God's creation, in essence must conform far and above his inanimate creations by instantaneous obedience in line with His will and Word.

James 1:22-25 encourages us to be doers and not hearers only, deceiving our own selves, and in verse 25 says whosoever looks at the perfect law of liberty shall be blessed in His ways. This is a guide that we should act upon God's Word appropriately and with focus on His instruction, which are perfect and is able to make us free indeed. If this is not the case, we act in forgetfulness of who we are as obedient children (1 Peter 1:14). Being children of God, God's Spirit ministers His will to our spirits (John 14:26). Also as His dear children in light (Colossians 1:12), we must therefore walk in the light of His Word (John 8:12, 12:35, Ephesians 5:8) and not in darkness (disobedience and in ignorance of His will and purpose) but to fulfill His will with precision. Also, being born anew, as His offspring and new breed, the ways of God becomes our mainstay and lifestyle, having been imparted with His life and nature (1 John 4:17).

Isaiah 59:21 (Amplified Bible) says, *"...My Spirit, Who is upon you [and Who writes the law of God inwardly on the heart]..."* God's spirit is within us and to do contrary to this nature is to severe the bond. God is our source, the foundation of our being. As our Creator and the essence of our being, complying absolutely with His will is only wise. As God's children, we cannot afford to live without constantly relating with His Spirit. This therefore means being alert and sensitive to His Spirit keeps us "alive". Obedience to His will preserves us in Him (Proverbs 19:16 NIV). As we do God's will instinctively, wilfully and timely, we demonstrate faith in God, thereby qualifying for His reward. Hebrews 11:6 says, *"But without faith it is impossible to please him: for he that cometh to God must believe that he is, and that **he is a rewarder** of them that diligently seek him."*

Basically therefore as God's children, we must recognise His voice and do His will. John 10:27 (NIV) says, *"My sheep listen to my voice; I know them, and they follow Me."* This meaning we must be quick to hear God and be swift to do as we have heard. The Bible says in 1 John 4:4 (NIV) that *"You, dear children, are from God and have overcome them, because the one who is in you is greater than the one who is in the world."* Since we are of God we must abide by His Word with all efforts and overcome all resistance to do so by the power of God that is at work in us. We must note that for us to be of God, means He owns everything about us inclusive of our time. This means in all we do, we must do at His time. It implies we do not live for ourselves but for God.

Jesus lived in the absolute will of the Father in aspects of life. Being one with God, He took the nature of man and as human, He obeyed the Father even through painful and difficult situation unto death. He complied solely and fully with the will of the Father in timely, instinctive and wilful obedience. By faith and confidence in the Father, He did not compromise.

Psalm 34:9 says, *"O fear the Lord, ye His saints, for there is no want to them that fear him."* We are preserved by trusting and obeying God. Reverential fear of God will make us avoid delay in doing God's will, a form of disobedience which denies us of God's result and God's reward. Reverence for God inspires our urgency and promptness in acting as specified. Punctuality and dedication are vital factors in our walk of obedience.

In 2 Corinthians 5:14 (GNT) it says, *"We are ruled by the love of Christ, now that we recognize that one man died for everyone, which means that they all share in his death."* Obedience demands sacrifice and selflessness. As Luke 9:61-62 explains, *"And another also said, Lord, I will follow Thee; but let me first go and bid them farewell, which are at home at my house 62. And Jesus said unto him, No man, having put his hand to the plough, and looking back, is fit for the kingdom of God."* What God require is full surrender and obedience without compromise. We therefore must tame our spirits to be in constant and absolute obedience in order to be entirely submitted to the Father. True love for The Father discerns and remains in His will.

Galatians 6:7-9 says, *"Be not deceived; God is not mocked: for whatsoever a man soweth, that shall he also reap. 8. For he that soweth to his flesh shall of the flesh reap corruption; but he that soweth to the Spirit shall of the Spirit reap life everlasting. 9. And let us not be weary in well doing: for in due season we shall reap, if we faint not."*

Song

Lord I live by Your Word
Lord I live by every Word from your mouth
I'm like a tree by the stream
I'm bearing fruits, my leaves are green
O Lord, I live by Your Word.

Chapter 3

In Determination

"Trust in the LORD with all your heart;
do not depend on your own understanding.
Seek his will in all you do,
and he will show you which path to take".
Proverbs 3:5-6 (NLT)

Job, who God vouched for his integrity, said in Job 23:10-12, *"But He knoweth the way that I take: when He hath tried me, I shall come forth as gold. 11. My foot hath held His steps, **His way have I kept, and not declined**. 12. **Neither have I gone back** from the commandment of His lips; **I have esteemed** the word of His lips mouth more than my necessary food"*.

The above portrays ardent obedience; it portrays great determination for obedience to the will of the Father. James 1:23-24 (NIV) says, *"Anyone who listens to the word but does not do what it says is like someone who looks at his face in a mirror* [24] and, after looking at himself, goes away and immediately forgets what he looks like." As we abide in God, He helps us. God has all things worked out for an ultimate purpose so we must obey God's instruction irrespective of situations. Disobedience will mean refuting the supremacy of God which carries its consequence. Deuteronomy 8:20 (NIV) *says "Like the nations the Lord destroyed before you, so you will be destroyed for not obeying the Lord your God."* It is wisdom to be importunate, pressing and persistent in acting in obedience to the will of the Father regardless of people or circumstance. Galatians 6:9 admonishes us not to be weary in well-doing. The Bible says in Proverbs 29:25, *"The fear of man bringeth a snare: but whoso putteth his trust in the LORD shall be safe."* We must always allow God's Word to decide our action above man's. Isaiah 51:7 says, *"Hearken unto me, ye that know righteousness, the people in whose heart is my law; fear ye not the reproach of men, neither be ye afraid of their reviling."* We must prevail over anything that wants to take the place of God and become our god instead. We should rather do away with what other 'gods' will have us do (Joshua 24:23-24).

In determination, give God first place, making constant effort to dominate every distraction by the flesh and any other pressures. Romans 13:14 (NIV) says, *"Rather, clothe yourselves with the Lord Jesus Christ, and do not think about how to gratify the desires of the flesh."* The Bible says that sin (disobedience) shall not have dominion over us (Romans 6:14). Dominate the lies and lust of the flesh, recognise the Spirit of God in you and let it prevail. 1 Peter 4:2 says, *"That he no longer should live the rest of his time in the flesh to the lusts of men, but to the will of God."*

Resist every fleshly restriction and any opposition in acting in obedience to God's will. Resist the flesh and the devil (James 4:7) for God resists the proud (that is the one who will not conform to His will) (James 4:6). For the Bible says in James 4:17, *"Therefore to him that knoweth to do good, and doeth it not, to him it is sin".* For God hates sin. In our determination to do the will of God we will find divine assistance. 1 Thessalonians

5:24 says, *"Faithful is he that calleth you, who also will do it."*

Obedience preserves while disobedience destroys and spoils things. Saul disobeyed God by resisting spiritual instruction through Samuel. 2 Chronicles 20:20 says, *"...Believe in the Lord your God, so shall ye be established; believe his prophets, so shall ye prosper."* Saul took things into his own hands, causing him to be annihilated and reversed from God. Disobedience causes our relationship with God to be remote. 2 Chronicles 24:19-20 (NIV) says, *"Although the Lord sent prophets to the people to bring them back to him, and though they testified against them, they would not listen.*[20] *Then the Spirit of God came on Zechariah son of Jehoiada the priest. He stood before the people and said, "This is what God says: 'Why do you disobey the Lord's commands? You will not prosper. Because you have forsaken the Lord, he has forsaken you."*

To obey completely, absolutely, fully and to the letter is what counts as obedience to God. Partial obedience is not obedience at all because what was prescribed or instructed has been violated (not wholesome or pure) so

God will not consider such as honour to Him. Absolute obedience is like offering spotless sacrifice without blemish or adulteration. In essence, absolute compliance in obedience brings absolute blessings. Luke 11:27-28 says, *"And it came to pass, as he spake these things, a certain woman of the company lifted up her voice, and said unto him, Blessed is the womb that bare thee, and the paps which thou hast sucked. But he said, Yea rather, blessed are they that hear the word of God, and keep it."*

King Saul violated God's instruction; he compromised, hence failing in obedience (1 Samuel 15:1-24). Looking at verse 3, Saul was given a clear and specific instruction: *"Now go and smite Amalek, and utterly destroy all that they have, and spare them not;"*

In verse 9 it says, *"But Saul and the people <u>spared Agag, and the best of the sheep, and of the oxen, and of the fatlings, and the lambs, and all that was good,</u> and would not utterly destroy them: but <u>every thing that was vile and refuse, that they destroyed utterly."</u>*

Saul's action was not absolute for sparing, leaving undone and not fully obeying because of what he considered acceptable to the people and to himself. God deemed Saul's action not as partial but as outright disobedience which we see in verse 20-24: *"And Saul said unto Samuel, Yea, I have obeyed the voice of the Lord, and have gone the way which the Lord sent me, and have brought Agag the king of Amalek, and have utterly destroyed the Amalekites.21 But the people took of the spoil, sheep and oxen, the chief of the things which should have been utterly destroyed, to sacrifice unto the Lord thy God in Gilgal.22 And Samuel said, Hath the Lord as great delight in burnt offerings and sacrifices, as in obeying the voice of the Lord? Behold, to obey is better than sacrifice, and to hearken than the fat of rams.23 For rebellion is as the sin of witchcraft, and stubbornness is as iniquity and idolatry. <u>Because thou hast rejected the word of the Lord, he hath also rejected thee from being king.</u>24 And Saul said unto Samuel, I have sinned: for I have transgressed the commandment of the Lord, and thy words: because I feared the people, and obeyed their voice."*

We see in verse 23 that disobedience cost Saul and his lineage the loss of the throne forever to David and his lineage. Saul was unlike David who in Psalm 16:11 said *"Thou wilt shew me the path of life: in thy presence is fulness of joy; at thy right hand there are pleasures for evermore"* and also unlike the man Job who in Job 23:10-12 (NLT) said, *"<u>For I have stayed on God's paths; I have followed his ways and not turned aside 12 I have not departed from his commands, but have treasured his words more than daily food</u>."*

As Children of God, His Word must be our sustenance.

Jesus commanded in Luke 6:36, *"Give and it will be given to you: good measure, pressed down, shaken together, and running over will be put into your bosom. For with the same measure that you use, it will be measured back to you."* When we obey God's command, the principle behind it automatically and eventually works for us. For the consequences of disobedience are damages which can be permanent, such as Saul's and the Israelites when they progressed in their journey without God (Numbers 14:40-45). Human justification is not tenable to God for violating

His Word. No reason is good enough to violate or disobey God. Pressure from people or the voice of the majority is not an excuse. Human rationalisation is not tenable to God; obedience has to be absolute and resolute. The Bible says in Proverbs 29:25, *"The fear of man brings a snare: but whoso puts his trust in the* Lord *shall be safe."* And in Psalm 118:8 it says, *"It is better to trust in the* Lord *than to put confidence in man."*

Disobedience can be very costly and without respite. It results in spoiling our relationship with God and, as we see of the Israelites, it made them vulnerable to attack and being brought into slavery in the hand of their enemies (Numbers 15:30-31). It is therefore safer to tolerate the demands of obedience than face the cost of compromising it. Hence we must always strive to ensure that our decision matches the will of God, in essence, we must be led by the Spirit of God (Romans 8:14).

Galatians 5:19-21 says, *"But if ye be led of the Spirit, ye are not under the law.19 Now the works of the flesh are manifest, which are these; Adultery, fornication, uncleanness, lasciviousness,20 Idolatry, witchcraft, hatred, variance, emulations, wrath, strife, seditions, heresies,21 Envyings, murders, drunkenness, revellings, and such like: of the which I tell you before, as I have also told you in time past, that they which do such things shall not inherit the kingdom of God."*

Paul keeps his flesh under strict control. He says in 1 Corinthians 9:27, *"But I keep under my body, and bring it into subjection: lest that by any means, when I have preached to others, I myself should be a castaway."* He recognises that the spirit and flesh are constantly at war and would not have his flesh prevail. It is when the flesh prevails that disobedience and other sins creeps in. He admonishes fellow Christians in Galatians 5:24-25 by saying, *"And they that are Christ's have crucified the flesh with the affections and lusts. 25 If we live in the Spirit, let us also walk in the Spirit."* In 1 Timothy 6:12, Paul says to *"Fight the good fight of faith, lay hold on eternal life."* Paul advises a good fight against all hindrances in a determined attempt to constantly be in obedience to God.

God's Word is perfect and must be honoured. There is no reason to violate, alter, modify or amend in order to suit the flesh. There is no justification or rationalisation that qualifies adjusting His word to suit any seemly permissible convenience. Saul's excuse in 1 Samuel 15 resulted in a violation of God's order. God demands outright and absolute obedience!

The Psalmist was confident saying God's Word is that lamp unto his feet and light to his path (Psalm 119:105) meaning that God's instructions gives him direction. It only implies that he will stick by it no matter how tough or unreasonable it may seem to him. He trusts God's Word to follow, knowing that by it he will not go astray. The Bible says God is faithful; His plans for us are good and not evil to give us a future and a hope (Jeremiah 29:11 NIV). Abraham moved at the first instance of God's direction quitting his land of birth for a place he did not know, trusting God to be the foundation of the strange new place. Without hesitation, determined to obey God though hard instruction, he moved while trusting that God would make a way. Hebrews 11:8-10 says, *"By faith Abraham, when he was called to go out into a place which he should after receive for an inheritance, <u>obeyed</u>; and* *he went out, not knowing whither he went.9 By faith he sojourned in the land of promise, as in a strange country, dwelling in tabernacles with Isaac and Jacob, the heirs with him of the same promise: 10 For he looked for a city which hath foundations, whose builder and maker is God."*

The Bible records that God counted this act of obedience as righteousness for Abraham. He was determined in honouring God with his obedience. He obeyed immediately, trusting God. By his act of faith and confidence in God he pleased God and he received credit for it. Just like Abraham we must dare to trust God, putting the grace of God to work in us.

In situations when our obedience is faced with contending forces, we must be even more determined, resolute, staunch, unbendable, unyielding, firm, stubborn, definite and unwavering to ensure that we please the Lord above all else. The ability required to do what God has instructed to be done is found in the doing. Peter was able to walk on water until he lost his focus on the Master (Matthew 14:28-30). God's word has the ability and power to produce what it talks about, therefore our solution is nowhere else but in acting upon the Word. Simply by embarking on God's Word, the power of God backs us up; not forgetting that we have a Standby (John 14:26 Amp). Be determined, launch into doing what God has commissioned you to do, be bold, be strong, be enthused from within you, and let the zeal for God drive you. It has to be done anyway, so be motivated and avoid disobedience. 1 John 5:3 (NLT) says, *"Loving God means keeping his commandments, and his commandments are not burdensome."* When God gives us instructions that are specific to us, He has already given us the capability. Moses gave God the excuse that he was a stutterer; he didn't consider that God, the One who knew him before approaching him with the task was also able to create empowerment for him before Pharaoh. He was not quick to remember that it was the same God who spared and channelled his life from being a homicide victim or slave child to being raised in the very home of the Pharaoh who killed the other boys of his age at birth.

The same can be said for Gideon, considered by God a mighty man of valour because God had already given him the capacity. What we know of these men was that God did not forsake them but saw them through. We must always realise that for every instruction, God has already given the ability (Hebrews 13:5-6, Luke 10:19, Acts 1:8, Romans 8:37, 1 John 4:4). Apostle Paul encouraged himself in this confidence in Philippians 4:13 by saying, *"I can do all things through Christ which strengtheneth me."*

The Bible tells us in 2 Corinthians 5:7 to should walk by faith and not by sight. The story in Luke 5:4-7 is another example for doing just as the Master would have us do, irrespective of circumstances. Luke 5:4-7 (NKJV) says, *"When He had stopped speaking, He said to Simon, "Launch out into the deep and let down your nets for a catch."5 But Simon answered and said to Him, <u>"Master, we have toiled all night and caught nothing; nevertheless at Your word I will let down the net."</u> 6 And **when they had done this,** they caught a great number of fish, and their net was breaking. 7 So they signaled to their partners in the other boat to come and help them. And they came and filled both the boats, so that they began to sink."*

Refuse to allow seemingly logical excuses stop you from witnessing the miracles that are possible as a result of depending and relying on God's capability and not your capacity, His ability and not your agility, His facility and not your anxiety. It is safer to do the will of God even if we cannot physically see logical reasons yet. Give it the extra effort of being in compliance with God's instruction. Simon could have said to Jesus, "Don't even bother, there is no point, this is something we have done all night long, forget it! It makes no sense wasting time over it all over again." This would have meant him and his team not witnessing the miracles that stirred them into following Jesus nor enjoyed the eventual spiritual opportunities and heights they all attained. Every Word spoken by God to us has the inherent power to do what it talks about. All that is required of us is the action of faith and confidence born out of determination to walk in obedience with God.

It would have been unwise of Simon to ignore the instruction of the Master. When God gives us an instruction it is to take us beyond our present level, it is to promote us. Sometimes the instruction does not come cheap or easy but we must always rely on the power that backs us up. Walking by faith and not by sight implies reliance on God. Stick with God no matter the situation and trust in Him. Never depend on sensory perception but on every Word from God. He is the God who can see the end from the beginning and the beginning from the end. He is the all-knowing God, the God of all flesh.

Jeremiah 32:27 says, *"Behold, I am the Lord, the God of all flesh. Is there anything too hard for Me?"*

I remember my husband once had the offer of two job contracts at the same time, both lasting three months. In thanksgiving for the two and with prayers for the right choice, he got the answer to go for the lower paid job offer and he obeyed. Amazingly and to the glory of God, three months after, the contract was renewed.

Month after month, this contract was rolled-over, unlike the other higher paid job which would have probably ended after the initial three months. He was also promoted, meaning he didn't have to hunt for contracts for three long years.

The Bible in Ephesians 5:10(Amp) says, *"And try to learn [in your experience] what is pleasing to the Lord [let your lives be constant proofs of what is most acceptable to Him]."* Obedience avails us the opportunity of experiencing or witnessing the miraculous.

In John 4:24 the Word of God states that *"God is a Spirit: and they that worship Him must worship Him in sprit and in truth."* The true worshipper, believer, disciple and offspring of God obeys as a necessary act of worship, a proof of relationship otherwise fellowship with His Spirit is mere empty speech (Luke 6:46). Our obedience honours God, it is our reasonable act of worship. True fellowship with God implies a spirit yielded. When we yield our spirits in submission to God's will, He in turn ministers back to our spirits the blessings of deep wisdom, knowledge and understanding derived from obedience (Ephesians 1:17-19). True wisdom knows what to do and does it. If we know that the Word of God is life and power, then we must also know that these are only acquired when the Word is acted upon.

Abraham worshipped and honoured God by being ardent, determined and dogged in obedience. He passed God's test, impressed God, and won God's approval, being ready to offer Isaac, the child he ever longed to have. Ready to sacrifice Isaac in outright and uncompromising obedience, Abraham accrued righteousness, gained scope and depth in relationship and in the knowledge and revelation of God coupled with many astounding generational reward and blessings. The Bible states in Hebrews 11:6 (Amp), *"But without faith it is impossible to please and be satisfactory to Him. For whoever would come near to God must [necessarily] believe that God exists and that He is the rewarder of those who earnestly and diligently seek Him [out]."* We see God state blessings of obedience to the Israelites in Leviticus 26:3-12.

In Genesis 14:21-15:7 we see Abraham in determination, with strength of mind and purposeful zeal in obedience to honour God. He was focused and determined in obedience for a rewarding life with God that transcended generations. Abraham focused on God's ability and not his and on God's capability and not his situation. He was dispassionate of circumstance, obedient to

God, he complied with the God who works all things out for good according to His purpose (Romans 8:28). He left the land of his birth, not knowing what followed but trusted and obeyed the God who truly rewards abundantly (Ephesians 3:20), making the once childless Abraham the father of many nations.

By this we see in Genesis 18:19 that Abraham's obedience won God's approval; with God attesting of him thus, *"For I know him, that he will command his children and his household after him, and they shall keep the way of the Lord, to do justice and judgment; that the Lord may bring upon Abraham that which he hath spoken of him."* No wonder, by obedient lifestyle in Abraham's seeds (generation) when God instructed Isaac not to quit Gerar the land wallowing in famine and ravished by poverty; he obeyed and stayed (Genesis 26:2-6). Considering that this was difficult and may not make sense to man, Isaac stayed and sowed and reaped in the same land of Gerar; he reaped multiplied harvests instead of enduring a famine and prospered greatly.

As Genesis 26:12-14 shows, *"Then Isaac sowed in that land, and received in the same year an hundredfold: and the Lord blessed him"13 And the man waxed great, and went forward, and grew until he became very great: 14 For he had possession of flocks, and possession of herds, and great store of servants: and the Philistines envied him."*

The Bible says in Isaiah 1:19 *"If ye be willing and obedient, ye shall eat the good of the land."* God's way is far above our way; His Words do not fail, the Bible says in Isaiah 55:8-11. Basically, in strict determination, we are to do the will of the Father who owns the ultimate plan for our lives.

Daniel and his friends, knowing these facts and also being confident that God's Word has efficacy and is infallible, above any intimidation acted in obedience to God and His ordinances and would not defile themselves in Babylon irrespective of any pleasure or pressure, offer or consequence; rather they stuck to their God. (Daniel 1:6-15). They recognised who they were and whose they were. Daniel 11:32 says, *"... but the people that do know their God shall be strong, and do exploits."* They were not intimidated.

In order to be exceptional in obedience like Daniel and his friends, we can ask God for the special grace to walk in supernatural obedience in the face of all odds. The Bible says to ask God our needs so our joy may be full. John 16:24 says, *"ask, and ye shall receive, that your joy may be full."* We have a promise in Ezekiel 36:27 that says, *"And I will put My spirit within you, and cause you to walk in My statutes, and ye shall keep My judgments, and do them."* As we allow God's Word to be our mainstay, our focus and the centre of our lives, we will not easily sway from our course with God but live in reverential fear and honour of His Words and thereby gain wisdom, understanding and insight.

Psalm 111:10 says, *"The fear of the Lord is the beginning of wisdom: a good understanding have all they that do his commandments..."* As we allow God's word to dwell in us richly by living the Word in all ramifications, we do not struggle in obedience but rather advance because we read it, do it, live it and speak the Word by walking the talk and talking the walk, making it our standard for life. Colossians 3:16 says, *"Let the word of Christ dwell in you richly in all wisdom; teaching and admonishing one another in psalms and hymns and spiritual songs, singing with grace in your hearts to the Lord."*

Paul was determined and committed in obedience to the faith even among nations (Romans 1:5, 16:25-26). He said that not all had obeyed the gospel but that those who have obeyed the truth have purified their souls (1 Peter 1:22). Jesus will bring vengeance on those who have not obeyed the gospel. Look in 2 Thessalonians 1:7-9, 1 Peter 4:17-18.

Be assured by Jesus that the Holy Spirit will be there for us. As helper John 14:18 says, *"I will not leave you comfortless: I will come to you."* This means we will not fail to have His guardian care. Isaiah 30:21 says, *"And thine ears shall hear a word behind thee, saying, this is the way, walk ye in it, when ye turn to the right hand, and when ye turn to the left."* It is in our own interest that we listen to and obey the guidance of our Helper. Wisdom is abiding in obedience with God no matter the circumstance, because He will never let us down. Matthew 28:20 says, *"...I am with you always, even unto the end of the world. Amen.*"

Since God is the One who created us and the only One who sees the future; our own plans therefore must submit to the plan He created us for, in order for His good and expected end. Jeremiah 29:11 says, *"For I know the thoughts that I think toward you, saith the* Lord, *thoughts of peace, and not of evil, to give you an expected end."* Therefore in obedience, act according to 1 Peter 5:6, "*Humble yourselves therefore under the mighty hand of God, that he may exalt you in due time.*"

Obedience is important so we may have life in its fullness. In John 10:10 (NIV) Jesus said, *"I have come that they may have life, and have it to the full."* We should never compromise obedience as it is better done afraid than not do it at all. Jeremiah 17:5 says," *Thus saith the Lord; Cursed be the man that trusteth in man, and maketh flesh his arm, and whose heart departeth from the Lord.*" And in Proverbs 29:25 *it says, "The fear of man bringeth a snare: but whoso putteth his trust in the Lord shall be safe.*"

Jonah feared the men of Nineveh and ended up regretting, the ten spies feared the Canaanites and therefore saw themselves as mere grasshoppers in other words, disenabling God's ability in them. The Word of God says the fear of men is a snare meaning it leads to bondage and incapacity. Men like Shadrach, Meshach and Abednego obeyed the Word of God and not other gods. They were not ensnared by the words of the king to bow to his image. Their obedience caused God Himself to deliver them from the fiery furnace (Daniel 3:11-30).

Joseph obeyed the Word of the Lord through the angel of the Lord not to fear but to take Mary, who was pregnant of the Holy Spirit, as his wife. Having obeyed gave him the privilege of being the earthly father of Jesus Christ (Matthew 1:20-25).

Only the fear of God should determine our actions and not the fear of men nor their perception of us. 1 Corinthians 7:23 says, "Ye *are bought with a price; be not ye the servants of men.*" This implies not being ruled or slaved by the opinion of men. Be determined. Proverbs 4:25-26 says, "*Let thine eyes look right on, and let thine eyelids look straight before thee. 26. Ponder the path of thy feet, and let all thy ways be established."*

I can testify that the Word of God is true and dependable. It is the life and light to our paths, to guard and to guide in line with God's perfect plan and purpose in order for an expected end.

I remember as a Pastor, in 2006 I was led by God to put together an inspirational workshop for women. Although I did not quite realize the reason for instruction at such a packed period in my life, having no choice, in surrender, I just simply obeyed.

The other thing the Lord said was for the event to be single-handedly sponsored by me without any other person's financial input or donation in offering.

On the day of event, an attendee, so concerned and touched by my actions, approached my assistant with a huge and beautiful bouquet of flowers and some cash for me in support and appreciation of my gesture in their community. Since I already informed my assistant of God's instruction, she collected only the flowers and in obedience nicely turned down the cash offer and reported to me. The lady with the offer insisted that it would alleviate my cost of hiring the venue but, by explaining in the best way possible, my assistant was eventually able to make her understand and respect my notion for the cash refusal.

Though I did not fully understand it at the time, I can say that eventually one major reward of obedience drawn from this experience was that I was launched by God to being able to run other bi-annual events single-handedly. I continued to self-sponsor community events and projects until God said otherwise and financial partners began to join in to support the various projects which have continue till today.

I remember that when The Lord revealed that I could receive support, I was careful in order not to be outside God's will, so I called my assistant to say what I thought I had heard God say. I noticed that she was very excited, because she too had received the same of God before but was rather reluctant to mention it to me in order to be quite sure.

I was elated by this confirmation. At the time God was preparing me for this new move, not only did God say that it was time to get financial support, He also assured me that He had prepared the people who would immediately support me, and this was so. Today, many people are happy supporting and witnessing the results of being part of the work.

Jesus our example demonstrated single-minded obedience. In determination to fulfill the will of the Father, He prayed. Luke 22:41-43. says, *"And He was withdrawn from them about a stone cast, and He kneeled down, and prayed, 42.saying, Father, if thou be willing, remove this cup from me: <u>nevertheless, not my will, but thine, be done. 43. And there appeared an angel unto Him from heaven, strengthening Him."</u>*

Jesus received strength for obedience. Thus when we are faced with struggle in doing God's will or we are in difficult situations that require our compliance with His will, we can pray for strength through obedience like Jesus so that the will of the Father be done.

2 Corinthians 5:21 says, *"For He hath made him to be sin for us, **who knew no sin**: that we might be made the righteousness of God in Him."* This was quite challenging for Jesus but through prayers He prevailed. In Philippians 2:8 the Bible says that He humbled himself and became obedient unto death, even the death on the cross. Considering that death on the cross is a most shameful and cruel one, Jesus obeyed the will of the Father to die the death of a criminal even though innocent. Jesus chose to be the sacrifice as the propitiation for our sins that the will of the Father be honoured in obedience; He became sin for us who knew no sin that we may become the righteousness of God (2 Corinthians 5:21).

Jesus was prepared to pay the price for God's will to be done. He obeyed even unto death since obedience is not carried out except it is done to precision. Delaying to understand God's reason before obeying amounts to disobedience. This is the reason we must abide in God and His ways in order to know Him, His ways and to be able to discern His will. In Luke 1:30-38 Mary the mother of Jesus did not understand it all when the angel told her she would conceive of the Holy Ghost and have a baby. *"And Mary said, Behold the handmaid of the Lord; <u>be it unto me according to thy word</u>."* We see Mary yield totally to the will of God.

We see the Psalmist too in Psalm 119:131, 167-168 determined for conformity with God's way, making a wilful decision for God's will to have the pre-eminence. Psalm 119:1-6(NIV) says, *"Blessed are those whose ways are blameless, who walk according to the law of the Lord. 2. Blessed are those who keep his statutes and seek him with all their heart — 3. they do no wrong but follow his ways. 4. You have laid down precepts that are to be fully obeyed. 5. Oh, that my ways were steadfast in obeying your decrees! 6. Then I would not be put to shame when I consider all your commands."* As God's children, we operate by His Word. Romans 8:14 says, *"For as many as are led by the Spirit of God, they are the sons of God".* Philippians 2:13 says, *"For it is God which works in you both to will and to do of his good pleasure."*

As God's children we are to allow ourselves to be ruled under the mighty hands of God for

His supreme plan for our lives as individuals to be fulfilled. When His Words rule and direct our lives, we are of the Spirit and not of the flesh. Those who are ruled of the flesh live by the senses, they are carnal and this means spiritual death (Romans 8:6). When we disobey we sever the relationship with God and break the seal and hedge of God's protection plan and provision.

To disobey is to give room to the devil and his scheme and because the Bible calls him the accuser of the brethren we must out-smart him so that even if he tries finding a case against us as he did Job, He may find none (Job 1:1-12). There is great safety in carrying out God's instructions as it will help us navigate through life victoriously. Job did not compromise in the face of turmoil but remained a conqueror. In being determined, no matter the cost of obedience, we derive great safety. If the Bible says that in all things give thanks (1 Thessalonians 5:18) then, whatever we receive from God to do will eventually end up in thanksgiving. Knowing this keeps us focused in doing the will of God since we know that all will turn out for our good (Romans 8:28). God's ultimate plans for us are good so we must not quench the Spirit or grieve the Holy Spirit (1 Thessalonians 5:19) because of disobedience but always yield to God's plan for us. Psalm 103:17-18 says, *"But the mercy of the Lord is from everlasting to everlasting upon them that fear him, and his righteousness unto children's children; 18 To such as keep his covenant, and to those that remember his commandments to do them."*

Just as Jesus has set us the example of humility and submission, we also must emulate Him in obedience. 1 Peter 5:6-9 enjoins us on this, so that God may exalt us in due season even as He did Jesus (Philippians 2:8-10). All we require is not to be apprehensive but to trust and cast our cares on God as we embark on our individual walk of obedience. Isaiah 26:3 says, *"Thou wilt keep him in perfect peace, whose mind is stayed on thee: because he trusteth in thee."*

Never be despondent also as you journey through obedience, for God is with you (Isaiah 41:10). Simply rely on His ability and not yours. In factual sense, fear should only occur in disobedience because it is a journey outside God's will. The Bible states in Proverbs 18:10 *"The name of the* LORD *is a strong tower: the righteous runneth into it, and is safe."* This is so as they are not outside of God's will and plan. They are therefore not susceptible to the devil's attack who the Bible warns us to resist steadfastly (James 4:7). The way to resist the devil and his allied pressure is by our dogged and ardent obedience to God's will and purpose. It is so important we stand our ground in obeying God regardless of the pressure and anxiety. We must ensure we remain unmoved in keeping to God's Word despite the opposition we face, for it pays to please God (Jeremiah 29:11, Romans 8:28, Ephesians 3:20) than succumbing to prevailing circumstance.

Abraham was rewarded for his focused obedience. Genesis 22:18 says, *"In your seed all the nations of the earth shall be blessed, because you have obeyed My voice."* Be unperturbed even when loved ones despise or ridicule your obedience. Matthew 5:11-12 says, *"Blessed are ye, when men shall revile you, and persecute you, and shall say all manner of evil against you falsely, for my sake. Rejoice, and be exceeding glad: for great is your reward in heaven...."* In the book of Acts, we read that the Apostles rejoiced despite being scourged by the Jews for preaching the Gospel. They were threatened never to preach the name of Jesus, yet the Bible recorded that they continued in faith with confidence in God. Apostle Paul said that he pressed in determination toward the mark for the prize of high calling of God in Christ Jesus (Philippians 3:14).

Whenever we find ourselves in situations contending with our obedience, we should simply resist the devil (James 4:7); meditate on God's Word and instruction, becoming focused and uncompromising. The Bible in Galatians 5:16 says, *"....Walk in the Spirit, and ye shall not fulfil the lust of the flesh."* Ephesians 6:13 instructs, *"Wherefore take unto you the whole armour of God, that ye may be able to withstand in the evil day, and having done all, to stand."* Peter and John found strength in order to obey God, even when threatened with death, as we can see in Acts chapter 4 where after calling on the name of Jesus to heal a man crippled for over 40 years, Peter and John were commanded by the religious leaders to stop speaking or teaching in the name of Jesus. Peter replied in Acts 4:19-20, *"....Whether it be right in the sight of God to hearken unto you more than unto God, judge ye. For we cannot but speak the things which we have seen and heard."*

Peter and John had resolved it in their hearts to obey and do exactly what Jesus had called them to do. We see their source of determination and boldness in Acts 5:29-32, *"Then Peter and the other apostles answered and said, <u>We ought to obey God rather than men.</u>30 The God of our fathers raised up Jesus, whom ye slew and hanged on a tree.31 Him hath God exalted with his right hand to be a Prince and a Saviour, for to give repentance to Israel, and forgiveness of sins.32 And we are his witnesses of these things; and so is also the **<u>Holy Ghost, whom God hath given to them that obey him</u>**."*

While on the other hand, we know what disobedience cost people like Lot's wife, Jonah, Saul, the Pharaoh and Egypt compared to the reward of obedience for people like Abraham, Isaac, Daniel and Jesus, to mention a few.

Sometimes responses to obedience may not make straight sense. For example, loving those who persecute us as the Word of God instructs in Matthew 5:43-45 is for an ultimate good purpose, that they may be drawn to God and not perish (2 Peter 3:9). It did not immediately make sense when Abraham obeyed to quit the land of his birth and sojourn in a strange land and for Isaac to stay in the land of famine, Gerar based on God's will but these two men discovered great prosperity in these lands as a result of determined obedience to God's Word.

Again the power of prayer to boost our determination to excel in obedience cannot be over-emphasised; Jesus did pray in this regard. Paul prayed for the Colossian Church in Colossians 1:9-13. He said, "For this cause we also, since the day we heard it, do not cease to pray for you, and to desire that ye might be filled with the knowledge of his will in all wisdom and spiritual understanding; *10That ye might walk worthy of the Lord unto all pleasing, being fruitful in every good work, and increasing in the knowledge of God; 11Strengthened with all might, according to his glorious power, unto all patience and*

<u>longsuffering with joyfulness;</u> 12Giving thanks unto the Father, which hath made us meet to be partakers of the inheritance of the saints in light: 13Who hath delivered us from the power of darkness, and hath translated us into the kingdom of his dear Son."

The power of prayer empowers us to do the will of the spirit over the wish of the flesh such that the will of the Lord prevails over our personal will. As we persist in prayers, God is ever willing to help with grace in time of need (Hebrews 4:16). As we do all these we must keep focused and determined by conscious action to suppress the flesh.

Romans 8:4-15 says, *"That the righteousness of the law might be fulfilled in us, who walk not after the flesh, but after the Spirit. 5For they that are after the flesh do mind the things of the flesh; but they that are after the Spirit the things of the Spirit. 6For to be carnally minded is death; but to be spiritually minded is life and peace. 7Because the carnal mind is enmity against God: for it is not subject to the law of God, neither indeed can be. 8So then they that are in the flesh cannot please God. 9But ye are not in the flesh, but in the*

Spirit, if so be that the Spirit of God dwell in you. Now if any man have not the Spirit of Christ, he is none of his. 10And if Christ be in you, the body is dead because of sin; but the Spirit is life because of righteousness. 11But if the Spirit of him that raised up Jesus from the dead dwell in you, he that raised up Christ from the dead shall also quicken your mortal bodies by his Spirit that dwelleth in you. 12Therefore, brethren, we are debtors, not to the flesh, to live after the flesh. 13For if ye live after the flesh, ye shall die: but if ye through the Spirit do mortify the deeds of the body, ye shall live. 14For as many as are led by the Spirit of God, they are the sons of God. 15For ye have not received the spirit of bondage again to fear; but ye have received the Spirit of adoption, whereby we cry, Abba, Father."

It is the will of God that we walk in righteousness according to His will, and He therefore makes His grace available for us. Hebrews 4:14-16 says, *"Seeing then that we have a great high priest, that is passed into the heavens, Jesus the Son of God, let us hold fast our profession. 15For we have not an high priest which cannot be touched with the* *feeling of our infirmities; but was in all points tempted like as we are, yet without sin. 16<u>Let us therefore come boldly unto the throne of grace, that we may obtain mercy</u>, and <u>find grace to help in time of need</u>."*

Just like us our Lord Jesus was tempted, but by grace and mercy available through prayer, he escaped disobedience. As offspring of God, love for the Father must keep us in obedience (Deuteronomy 11:1). His Word assures us the help in austere circumstances when situations contend with our obedience. Hebrews 3:14-15 says, *"For we are made partakers of Christ, if we hold the beginning of our confidence steadfast unto the end; 15While it is said, Today if ye will hear his voice, harden not your hearts, as in the provocation."*

In John 14:13-18 we have the assurance of His power, provision and presence: *"13And whatsoever ye shall ask in my name, that will I do, that the Father may be glorified in the Son. 14If ye shall ask any thing in my name, I will do it. 15If ye love me, keep my commandments. 16And I will pray the Father, and he shall give you another Comforter, that he may abide with you for ever; 17Even the Spirit of truth; whom the world cannot receive, because it seeth him not, neither knoweth him: but ye know him; for he dwelleth with you, and shall be in you. 18I will not leave you comfortless: I will come to you."*

All that we require is to live in acquiescence with the Father Who has bestowed unto us all that pertains to life and Godliness. 2 Peter1:3 says, *"According as his divine power hath given unto us all things that pertain unto life and godliness, through the knowledge of him that hath called us to glory and virtue".* By these, we therefore have the enablement to the Father's will and good pleasure as we see in Philippians 2:13 while verses 14-16 furnishes us with specific precautions: *"For it is God which worketh in you both to will and to do of his good pleasure. 14Do all things without murmurings and disputings: 15That ye may be blameless and harmless, the sons of God, without rebuke, in the midst of a crooked and perverse nation, among whom ye shine as lights in the world; 16Holding forth the word of life; that I may rejoice in the day of Christ, that I have not run in vain, neither laboured in vain."*

The Bible says in Psalm 112:1, *"Praise ye the Lord. Blessed is the man that feareth the* Lord, *that delighteth greatly in his commandments,"* and in Proverbs 15:31 that *"The ear that heareth the reproof of life abideth among the wise."* Proverbs 8:10 says that to *"Receive my instruction, and not silver; and knowledge rather than choice gold."* As God's children, it is therefore imperative that we conform to the will of the Father who deems us as peculiar people, a holy nation (1 Peter 2:9); a people separated unto Him.

Exodus 19:5 says, *"Now therefore, if ye will obey my voice indeed, and keep my covenant, then ye shall be a peculiar treasure unto me above all people: for all the earth is mine."*

The Bible also refers to us as His workmanship created in Christ Jesus unto good work (Ephesians 2:10). Not unto disobedience but unto the good work of obedience, just as Christ did. We receive this admonition in Romans12:2, "And be not conformed to this world: but be ye transformed by the renewing of your mind, that ye may prove what is that good, and acceptable, and perfect, will of God."

We see that our peculiar nature has it's expectation of us which should not be compromised in order that we may live the divine life in sync with the Father. The thing to do is to settle it in our hearts that nothing at all must make us disregard the Word of God. This is essential for the life we live and to be able to continue to live this peculiar life, will mean to perpetually submit and desire the Word (1 Peter 2:2) required for this quality and peculiar life.

No pressure, condition or sentiments must make us stoop in abiding by the Word. The result of obedience will always justify whatever it has cost us to obey. It is safe to obey rather than disobey and regret or be doomed. We must act on God's Word even if it means doing it afraid but never put situation or people above God's will, circumventing or operating in disparity with divine plan.

Do you live in line with our Maker's will? In Hebrews 10:7 and 9 it was written of Jesus our Perfect Model that He came to do and fulfill God's will. What about you? The preceding verse 6 depicts how our God our and Maker is not interested in offering and sacrifice which could mean alternatives but in obedience from a determined heart that is after His heart, will and purpose. Hebrews 10:7-9 (NLT) *says, "You were not pleased with burnt offerings or other offerings for sin.7 Then I said, 'Look, I have come to do your will, O God— as is written about me in the Scriptures.'" 8 First, Christ said, "You did not want animal sacrifices or sin offerings or burnt offerings or other offerings for sin, nor were you pleased with them" (though they are required by the law of Moses). 9 Then he said, "Look, I have come to do your will." He cancels the first covenant in order to put the second into effect."*

We must make up our minds and be determined like never before that nothing and no one will hinder us from conforming in strict obedience with the Father's will. Romans 12:2 (NIV) says, *"Do not conform to the pattern of this world, but be transformed by the renewing of your mind. Then you will be able to test and approve what God's will is – his good, pleasing and perfect will."* Decide that you will be ardent and quick to comply with God's Word and instruction, no matter what. This is important because your determination to obey in the face of opposition is a demonstration of faith and confidence in God, and in His ability to see you through and to recompense your obedience. Psalm 35:27 says, *"Let them shout for joy, and be glad, that favour my righteous cause: yea, let them say continually, Let the Lord be magnified, which hath pleasure in the prosperity of his servant.* And in Psalm 5:11 *"But let all those that put their trust in thee rejoice: let them ever shout for joy, because thou defendest them: let them also that love thy name be joyful in thee."*

God is faithful and if anything must matter to us, it must be giving obedience to Him and His Words first place. Jesus, who knew no sin, became sin for us. He was obedient to this will of the Father even unto a painful death on the cross in response to the Father's instruction to save a dying world. He was determined to fulfill the Father's will. Philippians 2:8 says, *"And being found in fashion as a man, he humbled himself, and became obedient unto death, even the death of the cross."* Jesus chose rather the will of the Father than to deny the cross. He was focused on God's will. In determination He did not quit, He complied in honour that divine plan and purpose be realised. We also, as fellow children of God, must live to fulfill the will of The Father. 2 Corinthians 5:15 (NLT) says, *"He died for everyone so that those <u>who receive his new life will no longer live for themselves. Instead, they will live for Christ</u>, who died and was raised for them."*

Jesus kept the flesh in subjection; even hunger could not make Him succumb and disobey. He said emphatically to the devil that man must not live by bread alone but by every Word from God, meaning the Word of God is food (to our spirit) which we must live by — a vital means of sustenance. Matthew 4:1-4 says *"Then was Jesus led up of the Spirit into the wilderness to be tempted of the devil.2 And when he had fasted forty days and forty nights, he was afterward an hungred.3 And when the tempter came to him, he said, If thou be the Son of God, command that these stones be made bread.4 But he answered and said, It is written, Man shall not live by bread alone, but by every word that proceedeth out of the mouth of God."*

The Bible make known to us in Romans 8:4-14, *"That the righteousness of the law might be fulfilled in us, who walk not after the flesh, but after the Spirit. 5For they that are after the flesh do mind the things of the flesh; but they that are after the Spirit the things of the Spirit. 6For to be carnally minded is death; but to be spiritually minded is life and peace. 7Because the carnal mind is enmity against God: for it is not subject to the law of God, neither indeed can be. 8So then they that are in the flesh cannot please God. 9But ye are not in the flesh, but in the Spirit, if so be that the Spirit of God dwell in you. Now if any man have not the Spirit of Christ, he is none of his. 10And if Christ be in you, the body is dead because of sin; but the Spirit is life because of righteousness. 11But if the Spirit of him that raised up Jesus from the dead dwell in you, he that raised up Christ from the dead shall also quicken your mortal bodies by his Spirit that dwelleth in you. 12Therefore, brethren, we are debtors, not to the flesh, to live after the flesh. 13For if ye live after the flesh, ye shall die: but if ye through the Spirit do mortify the deeds of the body, ye shall live.14For as many as are led by the Spirit of God, they are the sons of God."*

The flesh is designed to be subject to the spirit, for man is a spirit just as we see the scripture above (Romans 8:9). 1 Peter 2:2 says, *"As new-born babes, desire the sincere milk of the word, that ye may grow thereby."* The word of God is to be desired in obedience for our necessary spiritual growth and development.

So in this same vein, like Jesus we must be in strict determination for the will of the Father keeping the flesh from prevailing over our spirits. Obedience places us on a good stand with the Father, whenever the flesh tries to hinder us in conforming to God's instruction it must be quickly resisted. We must dominate our flesh such that our feelings and circumstances do not dictate. By obeying, we are kept in God's purpose.

Rebecca's brother, Laban and her father Bethuel mentioned to Abraham's servant that she was released to him to be Isaac's wife, based on obedience to God's will. Genesis 24:50-51 (NCV) says, *"Laban and Bethuel answered, "This is clearly from the Lord, and we cannot change what must happen. 51 Rebekah is yours. Take her and go. Let her marry your master's son as the Lord has commanded."* See how The Message Bible puts it: *"Laban and Bethuel answered, "This is totally from God. We have no say in the matter, either yes or no. Rebekah is yours: Take her and go; let her be the wife of your master's son, as God has made plain."*

Just as Jesus taught us in the Lord's Prayer in Matthew 6:10 *"Thy kingdom come, Thy will be done in earth, as it is in heaven,"* as God's children in the same image, we therefore must ensure strict compliance that the Father's will be done.

James 1:22-25 says, *"But be ye doers of the word, and not hearers only, deceiving your own selves. 23For if any be a hearer of the word, and not a doer, he is like unto a man beholding his natural face in a glass: 24For he beholdeth himself, and goeth his way, and straightway forgetteth what manner of man he was. 25But whoso looketh into the perfect law of liberty, and continueth therein, he being not a forgetful hearer, but a doer of the work, this man shall be blessed in his deed."*

One thing is sure, God honours determined obedience in honour of Him. Deuteronomy 5:10 says, *"And showing mercy unto thousands of them that love me and keep my commandments."*

God said to the Israelites in Deuteronomy 5:29-33, *"O that there were such an heart in them, that they would fear me, and keep all my commandments always, that it might be well with them, and with their children for ever! 30Go say to them, Get you into your tents again. 31But as for thee, stand thou here by me, and I will speak unto thee all the commandments, and the statutes, and the judgments, which thou shalt teach them, that they may do them in the land which I give them to possess it. 32Ye shall observe to do therefore as the LORD your God hath commanded you: ye shall not turn aside to the right hand or to the left. 33Ye shall walk in all the ways which the LORD your God hath commanded you, that ye may live, and that it may be well with you, and that ye may prolong your days in the land which ye shall possess."*

So that we are not a victim of disobedience, therefore we must be guided by God's Word in 1 Peter 5:8-9. The Bible mention in Revelations 3:21 of those who overcome the devil: *"To him that overcometh will I grant to sit with me in my throne, even as I also overcame, and am set down with my Father in his throne."* Hallelujah! What a faithful reward!

For resolute obedience like any other request, the Bible says for us to ask God, and as a genuine request, He will grant our request (Matthew 7:7). To receive enablement in determination to obey, there are responsibilities on our part:

- Earnestly determine to obey; making conscious, wilful and persistent effort towards it (Hebrews 2:1).
- Decide to be tough through obedience.
- Be apt and prompt to obey.
- Do not compromise obedience, be exact and appropriate.
- Resist giving up on obedience, never give up.
- Please God through it, not your flesh nor any man (Isaiah 51:7).

- Remember God is faithful to see you through.
- God is faithful to reward your obedience (Deuteronomy 11:13-15, Psalm 103:17-18).

With your determination, God is faithful to help you.

Ezekiel 36:27 says, *"And I will put my spirit within you, and cause you to walk in my statutes, and ye shall keep my judgments, and do them."*

Do not resist God will. Otherwise it is disobedience which translates to pride. This is detestable to God (James 4:6). In Philippians 2:8-9 we see that in spite of being Heaven's best, Jesus humbled Himself in order to conform to the will of the Father. He did not consider His esteemed self, thereby not allowing pride to stop Him; He related with the poor, the sinners and the down-trodden that the Father's will for their salvation be done. Like Jesus, we are humble ourselves to the will of the Father towards His purposed ultimate goal.

Reaching out to the less privileged, Jesus helped the sick, the poor, the sinners and the condemned, redeeming them with love — even those who hated him. James 4:6 says, *"But he gives more grace...."* It means as you embark on obedience, you receive grace to forge through.

Proverbs 23:26 says, *"My son, give me thine heart, and let thine eyes observe my ways."* We need to know God's Word in order to keep to His will. We must study it and meditate on it while ensuring that we abide in it. Joshua 1:8 says, *"This book of the law shall not depart out of thy mouth; but thou shalt meditate therein day and night, that thou mayest observe to **do according** to all that is written therein: for then thou shalt make thy way prosperous, and then thou shalt have good success."* The Bible enjoins us in Hebrews 2:1: *"Therefore we ought to give the more earnest heed to the things which we have heard, lest at any time we should let them slip."*

Obedience gives lasting blessings just as disobedience implies permanent damage. Romans 5:19 says, *"For as by one man's disobedience many were made sinners, so by the obedience of one shall many be made righteous."* Adam's disobedience alienated man from God but Jesus' sacrifice through obedience made man one with God. Jesus did not look at the process but proceeded to obey. We see this in Hebrew 12:2 *"Looking unto Jesus the author and finisher of our faith; who for the joy that was set before him endured the cross, despising the shame, and is set down at the right hand of the throne of God."*

He did not quit but focused on the finished work of obedience. Along our journeys of obedience we are privileged to look unto the Author and Finisher (Perfecter) for the strength through it, for the glory that will necessarily follow. 1 Peter 1:11 says, *"...and the sufferings of Christ, and the glory that should follow."* So, do not quit but receive strength (Isaiah 40:29-31) and wait to see God's expected end result and award.

Obedience is a qualification ticket, licence and authorisation to access God's blessings. Obedience brings you into deeper and fuller understanding and knowledge of God with intimacy. The more committed you are to

God in obedience, the more intimacy you will enjoy with Him. God rewards those who hold fast in doing His will, who give no room to excuses so as to adhere to His will (Revelations 3:8, 10-11). God takes pride in those who obey, as this portrays their faithfulness; He thus qualifies and edifies such for greater glories.

In Psalms 143:10 we see David make determined effort. He says, *"Teach me to do thy will; for thou art my God: thy spirit is good; lead me into the land of uprightness."* In determination too, we can make pronouncement for uprightness in the song below. The Word of God in Job 22:28 assures us that, *"Thou shalt also decree a thing, and it shall be established unto thee: and the light shall shine upon thy ways."*

Song

Breath on me breathe of God
Fill me with life anew
That I may love what Thou doth love
And do what Thou would do.

Chapter 4

It Pays

"For if I do this thing willingly, I have a reward:
but if against my will, a dispensation of the
gospel is committed unto me."
1 Corinthians 9:17

As creations of God, the manual by which we operate is the Bible, The Word of God for our instruction, to guide our operation through life. To operate in defiance to The Manual is to walk in destruction.

We must adhere to this Word for direction, observing it obediently for a fulfilling life (Proverbs 19:20). Operating by the Word results in the purpose of God as preordained for us as individuals. Our obedience keeps us in the path of God's good plan. Apostle Peter in 2 Peter 1:8 says, *"For if these things be in you, and abound, they make you that ye shall neither be barren nor unfruitful in the knowledge of our Lord Jesus Christ."* Simply put, Peter is saying that if we operate in virtue and it remains in us, aided by our obedience, we will be productive and full of great outcomes.

1 Corinthians 9:23-25 says, *"And this I do for the gospel's sake, that I might be partaker thereof with you.24 Know ye not that they which run in a race run all, but one receiveth the prize? So run, that ye may obtain.25 And every man that striveth for the mastery is temperate in all things. Now they do it to obtain a corruptible crown; but we an incorruptible."*

Obedience is rewarding, it gives the prize of a higher life to the doer (Philippians 3:14). When we find our obedience challenged in tough situations, the Bible promises in James 1:12 that, *"Blessed is the man that endureth temptation: for when he is tried, he shall receive the crown of life, which the Lord hath promised to them that love him."* God's Word in 1 Peter 5:10 also promises to settle us.

The prize of obedience outweighs the price. The price to pay in a situation of obedience may be difficult; or easy and seemingly naïve; but however it is, we must submit to God's instruction for His perfect will. For example Jehoshaphat was instructed by the Lord to put singers in front of the army at war front (2 Chronicles 20:15-30) and Joshua was instructed to get the Israelites to march round the wall of Jericho for it to crumble (Joshua 6:1-20). From these examples we see that it pays to obey God regardless and be fulfilled in the long run. In 1 Corinthians 1:27 we receive insight that God is in control of the universe and influences situations to dumbfound the world.

Basically and in essence The Word of God is for doing whether simple or otherwise, whether it makes sense to us or not. Rather than disobey because of present comfort or judgement based on sense knowledge or the flesh, it is more rewarding to face temporary discomfort than to miss out on eternal pleasure. As we will consistently remember the fact that God is in full control of the entire creation, bigger than everyone, everything and every situation; invariably casting our confidence in Him, trusting, relying, focusing and depending on Him in carrying out His will becomes easier.

Whether easy or not so easy, God's Word is to be acted upon in response to His perfect and supreme will. We know that for a product to perform at its premium capacity it must operate according to the manufacturer's instructions prescribed in its manual, otherwise it will malfunction or not perform optimally. In order to do well in life, for us as God's design or product, we must operate according His instruction for us. David said in Psalms 34:8, *"O taste and see that the LORD is good: blessed is the man that trusteth in him."* The Word of God, our Manual assures us support in Isaiah 40:31 and recompense in Deuteronomy 28:1 and verse 13 as well as in Isaiah 1:19.

Obedience paid off for Simon, James, and John, the sons of Zebedee — all fishermen who had toiled all night without a catch. Nevertheless, their obedience to the words of Jesus gave them the shock of their lives. From the same sea, they caught such a great multitude of fish that their nets began to break. We see this account in Luke 5 with

Simon's responsive attitude. *"And Simon answering said unto him, Master, we have toiled all the night, and have taken nothing: nevertheless at thy word I will let down the net."* He obeyed regardless of the prevailing contrary situation. They were already washing their nets, ready to quit, but by reason of obedience, the same lake in which they caught no fish produced to them a result and reward. *"And when they had this done, they enclosed a great multitude of fishes: and their net brake.7 And they beckoned unto their partners, which were in the other ship, that they should come and help them. And they came, and filled both the ships, so that they began to sink."*

2 Corinthians 10:5 states, *"Casting down imaginations, and every high thing that exalteth itself against the knowledge of God, and **bringing into captivity every thought to the obedience of Christ;** And having in a readiness to revenge all disobedience, **when your obedience is fulfilled.**"*

We see the case of Elijah's obedience too in 1 Kings 17:3-6: *"Get thee hence, and turn thee eastward, and hide thyself by the brook*

Cherith, that is before Jordan.4 And it shall be, that thou shalt drink of the brook; and I have commanded the ravens to feed thee there.5 So he went and did according unto the word of the Lord: for he went and dwelt by the brook Cherith, that is before Jordan.6 And the ravens brought him bread and flesh in the morning, and bread and flesh in the evening; and he drank of the brook". These two instances portray power being released as outcome or result of obedient actions. The Bible has it in Isaiah 1:19 that, *"If ye be willing and obedient, ye shall eat the good of the land."*

Jesus conformed to the will of the Father and won the Father's recompense. Philippians 2:8-9 says, *"And being found in fashion as a man, he humbled himself, and became obedient unto death, even the death of the cross.9 Wherefore God also hath highly exalted him, and given him a name which is above every name."*

When we trust God, giving Him room through our obedience; not trusting in the things created by Him which the Bible refers to as uncertain riches in 1 Timothy 6:17, then, we are told He gives us all things richly to enjoy.

We have these assurances in God's Word. Psalm 146:5-6 states, *"Happy is he that hath the God of Jacob for his help, whose hope is in the Lord his God: 6 Which made heaven, and earth, the sea, and all that therein is: which keepeth truth for ever: 8 For he shall be as a tree planted by the waters, and that spreadeth out her roots by the river, and shall not see when heat cometh, but her leaf shall be green; and shall not be careful in the year of drought, neither shall cease from yielding fruit."*

Every act of obedience is pregnant with blessing which is only delivered when fully carried out. The Word of God is the wisdom; it promotes, brings blessings and honours unlike disobedience which, as we see, destroys in the case of Achan in the book of Joshua chapter 7.

Obedience is imperative for us as God's children in order to earn His blessings. Proverbs 16:15 (TLB) says, *"Many favours are showered on those who please the king,"* and in Proverbs 16:20 (TLB) it says, *"God blesses those who obey him: happy is the man who puts his trust in the Lord."*

Indeed obedience pays. The Israelites were going to possess Abraham's blessing by obeying God (Deuteronomy 8:6-18) and they had to work at it by a relationship of compliance with God. Giving God an all-round free-hand on all issues delivers to us a great prize.

I remember having a particular phone that was serving me quite well, but it was not quite up-to-date. I had the leading by the Spirit to upgrade it and, thinking it was just a fashion issue and not wanting to be superficial, I continued with this phone for many weeks.

I was of the assumption that trend does not matter much to God, but surprisingly this nudge continued about upgrading the phone (God knew for the work required of me for the next level, I needed advanced tool) I considered getting an electronic pad (epad) instead since I had a phone. (But God, all-knowing had a reason for a smart phone.)

I then acted accordingly, got the phone but while trying to get used to it I exhibited subtle attitudes that caused me to think, 'but I was

okay with the former phone what is all this?'
The good thing is God is patient and kind.
My ignorance didn't matter, but His provision
that was laden with good things was what
mattered.

When I got used to this new phone, my work
and planning became far easier, I couldn't be
more grateful. It did not end there, the epad
I desired above the phone was presented to
me as a gift few months later. God knew all
the while!

As I unwrapped the epad, I was humbled,
I really was, I went prostrate, face to the
ground and awed like never before God. I
am sure God had a good laugh at me on that
day. I am glad that I obeyed.

Brothers and sisters let us obey and trust
the God who is all-knowing, knowing the
beginning from the end and the end from
the beginning. Let us allow ourselves to
be processed through obedience unto
fulfillment. When we make God final arbiter
in our lives, He will take control of everything
about us both great and small for He is
ever so faithful, ever so sure. The popular

Hymn says, '....morning by morning new mercies I see, all I have needed Thy hands have provided. Great is thy faithfulness Lord unto me.'

God wants us to live above the circumstances of this world which are threats to the safe delivery of the blessings of obedience. Psalm 84:5 says, *"Blessed is the man whose strength is in Thee; in whose heart are the ways of them."* Abraham's obedience in Genesis 22:1-3 and its result 15-18 reassures us that obedience is rewarding: *"And it came to pass after these things, that God did tempt Abraham, and said unto him, Abraham: and he said, Behold, here I am.2 And he said, Take now thy son, thine only son Isaac, whom thou lovest, and get thee into the land of Moriah; and offer him there for a burnt offering upon one of the mountains which I will tell thee of.3 And Abraham rose up early in the morning, and saddled his ass, and took two of his young men with him, and Isaac his son, and clave the wood for the burnt offering, and rose up, and went unto the place of which God had told him.* In Genesis 15-18 *"And the angel of the Lord called unto Abraham out of heaven the second time,16 And said, By myself have*

I sworn, saith the Lord, for because thou hast done this thing, and hast not withheld thy son, thine only son:17 That in blessing I will bless thee, and in multiplying I will multiply thy seed as the stars of the heaven, and as the sand which is upon the sea shore; and thy seed shall possess the gate of his enemies;18 And in thy seed shall all the nations of the earth be blessed; because thou hast obeyed my voice."

Never ignore the nudge or prompt from within, Philip did not (Acts 8:29-30). Learn to heed to the whisper of the Holy Spirit our Helper to keep us in check, in line with The Father's will. It is to our advantage that we respond, for as we heed the Spirit of God, the more attuned we will be to divine instructions. Therefore be resolute in yielding to the Spirit for divine directions by obedient response. To ignore divine assistance is to lose track. The Bible says in Proverbs 4:22 that His Words are life to those that find them (who discover; hear and do them). In Proverbs 3:1-2 (NKJV) it says, *"My son, do not forget My law, but let your heart keep My commands; 2. For length of days and long life and peace they will add to you."*

Peace of mind is one of God's recompense for obedience. To be out of the will of our Creator can be regrettable. Proverbs 1:24-27 (NIV) says, *"But since you rejected Me when I called and no one gave heed when I stretched out My Hand, 25. since you ignored all My advice and would not accept my rebuke, 26. I in turn will laugh at your disaster; I will mock when calamity overtakes you 27. when calamity overtakes you like a storm, when disaster sweeps over you like whirlwind, when distress and trouble overwhelms.* "It is wisdom when we comply with God than to disobey and be outside His original intention for us.

Our true faith and trust in God is demonstrated and evident by our obedience. A life of enduring and perpetual obedience brings about secured and victorious life; life lived far above the devil's antics and machinations since it is hinged on God's directives, His Word and guidance. The obedience life qualifies for the higher things in God. Jeremiah 17:7-8 states, *"Blessed is the man that trusteth in the Lord, and whose hope the Lord is. 8. For he shall be as a tree planted by the waters, and that spreadeth out* her roots by the river, and shall not see when heat cometh, but her leaf shall be green; and shall not be careful in the year of drought, neither shall cease from yielding fruit."

The Psalmist desired to do God's will, making his request in Psalm 27:11, *"Teach me Thy way, O Lord and lead me in a plain path, because of mine enemies"*. He knew that in doing the will of God there is safety. In Psalm 112:1-3 he could confidently say, *"Praise ye the Lord. Blessed is the man that feareth the Lord, that <u>delighteth greatly in his commandments</u>. 2. His seed shall be mighty upon earth: the generation of the upright shall be blessed. 3.Wealth and riches shall be in his house: and his righteousness endureth for ever."*

In the same light did Apostle Paul speak to the Ephesians elders in Acts 20:32 (TLB): *"And now I entrust you to God and His care and His wonderful Words which are able to build your faith and give you all the inheritance of those who are set apart for himself."*

Paul in his letter in Philippians 2:13-17 says, *"For it is God which worketh in you both to* *will and to do of His good pleasure. 14. Do all things without murmuring and disputing. 15.That ye may be blameless and harmless, the sons of God, without rebuke, in the midst of a crooked and perverse nation, among whom ye shine as lights in the world; 16. <u>Holding forth the word of life</u>; that I may rejoice in the day of Christ, that I have not run in vain, neither laboured in vain."*

Obedience to God means to see and do things from His perspective. It paid Abraham and his generations off and they prospered greatly. The Bible in Hebrews 11:6 tells us that God is a Rewarder of those that diligently seek Him. In verse 8 we see of Abraham that regardless of how daunting and tough it was, having to leave the land of his birth, not knowing anything about where he was going, to sojourn in a totally strange land, he still obeyed. In verse 17, we see how he continued in a life of obedience with God, offered up his son in outright obedience, all of which qualified Abraham as a friend of God (Genesis 18:17-19, James 2:23), qualified Him for God's abundant blessings (Genesis 13:2) and brought him a reward as father of many nations (Genesis 17:3-8). Considering all these, we see Abraham deservingly earning these rewards of obedience.

It is advisable for us as Christians to let God's Word direct us no matter the situation, just like Jesus who, regardless of all (Philippians 2:5-10), stopped at nothing but was obedient unto death, gaining God's recompense. As God's children we also, must ensure that our obedience withstands life's tests so we may gain God's reward (Hebrew 11:6). If in humility we comply in obedience to the will of God, His Word in 1 Peter 5:6 assures that He will exalt us in due time.

The more we submit in obedience to God, the more out of trust He will commit greater things into our hands to our own advantage. The more we build our relationship with God through obedience, the deeper and richer and the more intimate our fellowship with Him.

The Bible says deep calls unto deep (Psalms 42:7). In essence, the deeper you are in doing God's bidding, the deeper He relates with you in the things of the Spirit and the more you bond and get habituated with His way.

The more Abraham passed God's test of obedience, the more God trusted him and committed to him the deeper things and the more his relationship with God grew. Abraham proved and demonstrated love for God by ardent obedience. We prove we love God when we do His will and God is so faithful to reciprocate. John 14:23 record Jesus saying. *"If a man love Me, he will keep My Words: and My Father will love him, and we will come unto him, and make our abode with him."*

The book of Joshua 1:8-9 encourages us to observe to do according as written in the Word of God for our ways to be prosperous and also to have good success and that God will be with us in the situation. Obeying the Word of God by following and doing it as directed and instructed though His Word and by His Spirit brings lasting peace and assurance. The Bible says in Roman 8:1 that there is now no condemnation to them which are in Christ Jesus, who walk not after the flesh, but after the Spirit (His direction, will, plan and purpose). Revelation 3:8 states, *"I know thy works: behold, I have set before thee an open door, and no man can shut it: for* *thou hast a little strength, and <u>hast kept my</u> <u>Words</u>, and hast not denied My name.* "This interprets recompense of obedience with an open door, implying boundless opportunities without restrictions.

The blessings of walking in obedience with God are numerous. Every instruction carries with it its blessings. Response to God in obedience always eventually unveils its lasting benefit. Job 36:11 says, *"If they obey and serve Him, they shall spend their days in prosperity, and their years in pleasure."*

To simply obey God, simply doubt your doubts; for God never fails (Deuteronomy 7:9). Anyone in obedience is in sync with God in spirit and in truth for the Bible says God seeks such to worship Him (John 4:23). To worship God requires reverence and obedience.

Psalm 128 narrates the blessings of the man who fears the Lord in reverence, who honours His Word and His ways to observe them: *"Blessed is every one that feareth the LORD; that walketh in his ways. 2For thou shalt eat the labour of thine hands: happy shalt thou be, and it shall be well with thee. 3Thy wife shall be as a fruitful vine by the sides of thine house: thy children like olive plants round about thy table. 4Behold, that thus shall the man be blessed that feareth the LORD. 5The LORD shall bless thee out of Zion: and thou shalt see the good of Jerusalem all the days of thy life. 6Yea, thou shalt see thy children's children, and peace upon Israel."*

God honours those who honour His will. Ephesians 5:1 says, *"Be ye therefore followers of God, as dear children."* Disobeying means being out of sync with God which implies sin and the Bible says in Romans 6:14 that sin shall not have dominion over us. The one who is in sync with God is blessed and walking in His perfect plan, daily loaded with His benefits (Psalm 68:19). God renews his strength for greater things and take such from level to level and from glory to glory. Psalms 31:23-24 says, *"O love the LORD, all ye his saints: for the LORD preserveth the faithful, and plentifully rewardeth the **proud doer**. 24Be of good courage, and he shall strengthen your heart, all ye that hope in the LORD."*

There are many rewards for the doer of the Word. 1 John 3:22 says, *"And whatsoever we ask, we receive of him, because we keep his commandments, and do those things that are pleasing in his sight."* Psalm 103:17-18 says, *"But the mercy of the Lord is from everlasting to everlasting upon them that fear him, and his righteousness unto children's children; 18 To such as keep his covenant, and to those that remember his commandments to do them."*

It is important we develop our faith and confidence in God as it boosts our level of obedience. Obedience may not be easy in some circumstances but it is well worth it. Simply rely on God, independent of our circumstances, in such situations. Our confidence in God aids our obedience. As we follow through obedience in difficult or tough situations, we allow God to form us for higher things.

We see the Psalmist rely on God in Psalm 121. He says, "I will lift up mine eyes unto the hills, from whence cometh my help. *2 My help cometh from the Lord, which made heaven and earth. 3 He will not suffer thy foot to be moved: he that keepeth thee will not slumber. 4 Behold, he that keepeth Israel shall neither slumber nor sleep.5 The Lord is thy keeper: the Lord is thy shade upon thy right hand.6 The sun shall not smite thee by day, nor the moon by night.7 The Lord shall preserve thee from all evil: he shall preserve thy soul.8 The Lord shall preserve thy going out and thy coming in from this time forth, and even for evermore."*

Isaiah 43:2 says *"When thou passest* through the waters, I will be with thee; and through the rivers, they shall not overflow thee: when thou *walkest* through the fire, thou *shalt not be burned; neither shall the flame kindle upon thee."*

Joshua 1:8 *"This book of the law shall not depart out of thy mouth; but thou shalt meditate therein day and night, that thou mayest observe to do according to all that is written therein: for then thou shalt make thy way prosperous, and then thou shalt have good success."*

Hebrews 4:12 says *"For the word of God is quick, and powerful, and sharper than any two-edged sword, piercing even to the dividing asunder of soul and spirit, and of the joints and marrow, and is a discerner of the thoughts and intents of the heart."*

With Scriptures like these in our hearts and mouths, our confidence is stimulated in resolute obedience.

At times, obedience is a seed, a type of necessary sacrifice. Psalms 126:6 says, *"He that goeth forth and weepeth, bearing precious seed, shall doubtless come again with rejoicing, bringing his sheaves with him."* God always works out all situations, convenient or not, difficult or not as long as it is in accordance with His will, together for our good. Romans 8:28 says, *"And we know that all things work together for good to them that love God, to them who are the called according to his purpose."*

Certainly, it does work together for our good. God does not fail, He will never leave us nor forsake us (Hebrews 13:5) and since God rewards obedience, a demonstration of faith in His ability, He sees us through. Our obedience is important to God and as a Father; God will want us to *"Apply your heart to instruction and your ears to words of knowledge."* (Proverbs 23:12). As we walk in the path of obedience, we activate the power of God's Spirit to back us up in the situation.

To be obedient is to live a life of discretion given that we are anchored to God's leading. Abraham honoured God's word not to get Isaac a wife from where he sojourned in Canaan but from his original native land Nahor. Obeying God and trusting God enough, Abraham sent his servant in search for a wife for his son Isaac in obedience to God's instruction.

Obedience depicts your fervour and delight for the Lord. As we delight in doing God's will, God delights also in us and He is attentive to our prayers. Isaiah 58:14 says, *"Then shalt thou delight thyself in the* Lord*; and I will cause thee to ride upon the high places of the earth, and feed thee with the heritage of Jacob thy father: for the mouth of the* Lord *hath spoken it."*

Wisdom is doing the Father's will; to do His will is to walk according to His pre-ordained plan. He created the whole universe and He is in full control of all things. To live out His Word is to remain surely engrafted in Him. Proverbs 4:13 says, *"Take fast hold of instruction; let her not go: keep her; for she is thy life."*

Psalms 143:10 says, *"Teach me to do thy will; for thou art my God: thy spirit is good; lead me into the land of uprightness."* Wisdom is to constantly seek to do the will of the Lord and to obey Him in strict fervency. There is power, victory and dominion received in acting upon the Word of God; a demonstration that is a proof of our love for the Lord. Ecclesiastes 8:5 says, *"Whoso keepeth the commandment shall feel no evil thing: and a wise man's heart discerneth both time and judgment. "*This means he knows what to do and therefore is importunate in obedience. When God asks you to do anything, simply just go ahead, do not let fear cripple nor stop you. Caste your confidence in the unfailing God and JUST DO IT!

Jesus made a profound statement in Luke 6:46 *"And why call ye me, Lord, Lord, and do not the things which I say?"* The Bible says in

1 John 4:18 that fear has torment and fear is of the devil. The Bible says in James 4:7 to resist the devil. Rather than please the devil and displease God, do it still in 'the fear' letting God find you in it (in obedience); Who is faithful to see you through (Hebrews 13:5). Hebrews 11:6 says, *"But without faith it is impossible to please him: for he that cometh to God must believe that he is, and that he is a rewarder of them that diligently seek him."* Surely, God will meet you in the situation, He met Abraham in his when Isaac was about to be sacrificed.

Is your situation challenging? What pointers are you receiving through God and His Word, for you to act upon? Never forget we serve The ALMIGHTY God, the God of EVERYTHING, who made everything, knows everything and CAN HANDLE ANYTHING! Do not be dismayed nor be discouraged. Through trusting and depending on God, David fixed His 'Goliath' (challenge).

Deuteronomy 6:3 says, *"Hear therefore, O Israel, and <u>observe to do it</u>; <u>that it may be well with thee</u>, and <u>that ye may increase mightily</u>, as the LORD God of thy fathers hath promised* *thee, in the land that floweth with milk and honey."*

Deuteronomy 6:25 adds, *"And it shall be our righteousness, <u>if we observe to do all these commandments before the LORD our God</u>, as he hath commanded us."*

You are His 'Israel' today. "I will never leave nor forsake" are His Words of assurance to you, THEREFORE OBEY!

Galatians 6:9 says, *"And let us not be weary in well doing: for in due season we shall reap, if we faint not."*

Deuteronomy 7:9 says, *"Know therefore that the LORD thy God, he is God, the faithful God, which keeps covenant and mercy with them that love him and keep his commandments to a thousand generations."*

And in Deuteronomy 7:12-18 it adds, *"Wherefore it shall come to pass, if ye hearken to these judgments, and keep, and do them, that the LORD thy God shall keep unto thee the covenant and the mercy which he sware unto thy fathers: 13And he will love thee, and bless thee, and multiply thee: he will also bless the fruit of thy womb, and the fruit of thy land, thy corn, and thy wine, and thine oil, the increase of thy kine, and the flocks of thy sheep, in the land which he sware unto thy fathers to give thee. 14Thou shalt be blessed above all people: there shall not be male or female barren among you, or among your cattle. 15And the LORD will take away from thee all sickness, and will put none of the evil diseases of Egypt, which thou knowest, upon thee; but will lay them upon all them that hate thee. 16And thou shalt consume all the people which the LORD thy God shall deliver thee; thine eye shall have no pity upon them: neither shalt thou serve their gods; for that will be a snare unto thee. 17If thou shalt say in thine heart, These nations are more than I; how can I dispossess them? 18Thou shalt not be afraid of them: but shalt well remember what the LORD thy God did unto Pharaoh, and unto all Egypt."*

God blesses the act of obedience. Proverbs 14:23 says that in all labour there is profit. God spelt out the outcome of obedience and disobedience to the Israelites in Leviticus 26:3-39. The effect of our action has its ripple and lasting effect. Romans 5:19 says, *"For as by one man's disobedience many were made sinners, so by the obedience of one shall many be made righteous."* The effect of the disobedience of Adam alienated man from God and the obedience of Christ made salvation possible.

Our obedience opens up channels of lasting blessing. Many generations after Abraham partook of his blessing. Abraham was devoted to God; he demonstrated trust in God by obedience through submission to His instructions, he being ready to give up Isaac. Having pleased God, He counted it righteousness (Romans 4:22).

Obedience means submission and it implies respect because doing the will of God implies giving Him honour. By obedience we avail ourselves of actions that builds deeper in trust and confidence in God because as we witness the result and miracles while doing God's will, we move from level to level and get deeper and deeper in God and His ways.

There is also security and God's rest in obedience. Obedience brings God's reward.

Hebrews 4:1-3 says, *"Let us therefore fear, lest, a promise being left us of entering into his rest, any of you should seem to come short of it. 2For unto us was the gospel preached, as well as unto them: but the word preached did not profit them, not being mixed with faith in them that heard it. 3For we which have believed do enter into rest, as he said, As I have sworn in my wrath, if they shall enter into my rest: although the works were finished from the foundation of the world."*

Disobedience which is the rejection of the Word of God or His instructions is to walk in darkness instead of light, confusion, instead of peace and order. Psalms 82:5 says, *"They know not, neither will they understand; they walk on in darkness: all the foundations of the earth are out of course."*

David made a profound declaration in Psalms 119:106. He said, *"I have sworn, and I will perform it, that I will keep thy righteous judgments."* No wonder in Psalms 34:7-11 he has this to say: *"The angel of the LORD encampeth round about them that fear him, and delivereth them. 8 O Taste and see that the LORD is good: blessed is the man that trusteth in him. 9 O fear the LORD, ye his saints: for there is no want to them that fear him 10 The young lions do lack, and suffer hunger: but they that seek the LORD shall not want any good thing. 11 Come, ye children, hearken unto me: I will teach you the fear of the LORD."*

Wisdom is abiding in obedience. God's Word to His children are, "I will never leave nor forsake you." (Hebrews13:5). Jesus promised His presence with us in John 14:15-16 (Amp): *"If you [really] love Me, you will keep (obey) My commands. 16And I will ask the Father, and He will give you another Comforter (Counselor, Helper, Intercessor, Advocate, Strengthener, and Standby), that He may remain with you forever."*

We have the blessing of answers to prayers when we walk in obedience. John 15:7 says, "If *ye abide in me, and my words abide in you, ye shall ask what ye will, and it shall be done unto you."*

It pays to obey. In Psalm 119:99-100 the Psalmist says, *"I have more understanding than all my teachers: for thy testimonies are* *my meditation.100 I understand more than the ancients, <u>because I keep thy precepts</u>"* and in Psalm 119:112 *"I have inclined mine heart to perform thy statutes <u>alway, even unto the end</u>."*

It pays to listen to and abide in doing God's will for lasting blessing. Deuteronomy 6:2 (NIV) says, *"So that you, your children and their children after them may fear the Lord your God as long as you live by keeping all his decrees and commands that I give you, and so that you may enjoy long life."* We see this happen in Genesis 26:12-14 when Isaac, son of Abraham sowed in a famine land and prospered greatly.

Psalm 112:1-3 says, *"Praise ye the Lord. Blessed is the man that feareth the Lord, that delighteth greatly in his commandments.2 His seed shall be mighty upon earth: the generation of the upright shall be blessed.3 Wealth and riches shall be in his house: and his righteousness endureth for ever."*

I remember someone narrating her story of obedience, who having received a number of disrupted calls from her sister, which meant her calling back (as a matter of courtesy and consideration), but could not, because of the nudge within her not to do so at the time. She mentioned not understanding the reason for this usual reaction and the resistance she felt but decided she was just going to comply (John 10:27).

It was later that this sister she was meant to call back told her that the calls she had received were not intentional but accidental calls due to movement over her concealed phone while armed bandit ransacked her. In determined not to lose her prestigious and new phone, she did not disclose to the bandits despite threats. This meant that if her sister had rung back, the bandits would have discovered she had a phone on her which she wasn't surrendering. This meant additional trouble for being stubborn coupled with losing the phone.

She praised and acknowledged her sister's obedience and her alertness to the Spirit which had saved her and her treasured gadget.

John 14:16 -18 says, *"And I will pray the Father, and he shall give you another Comforter, that he may abide with you forever; 17 Even the Spirit of truth; whom the world cannot receive, because it seeth him not, neither knoweth him: but ye know him; <u>for he dwelleth with you, and shall be in you.</u>18 <u>I will not leave you comfortless: I will come to you.</u>"* Meaning He will not leave us without support and assistance. If He is abiding with us, we will constantly hear from Him, teaching and guiding us (John 14:26). It is therefore wisdom to stick with hearing and doing as the Father; the Counsellor, Teacher and Helper will direct or instruct in order for our safety and success.

As we constantly choose to obey, it will eventually become a lifestyle so that we find ourselves no longer having to struggle but producing fruits. Acts 20:32 *says "....the word of his grace, which is <u>able to build you up</u>, and to give you an inheritance among all them which are sanctified."*

Apostle Paul sought to bring about the 'obedience to the Faith' among the nations (Romans 1:5, 16:25-26). We see what Peter had to say about those who have purified their souls obeying the truth (1 Peter 1:22-23), and those who have not (2 Thessalonians 1:8-9).

This sets the contrast with those who have obeyed, overcoming temptation, keeping the Word, who will partake of God's blessings. Revelations 2:26-28 says, *"And he that overcometh, and keepeth my works unto the end, to him will I give power over the nations: 27And he shall rule them with a rod of iron; as the vessels of a potter shall they be broken to shivers: even as I received of my Father. 28And I will give him the morning star."*

God is gracious. The good news is that out of His mercy, even if we have missed it at one point or the other, the Bible says that God is just and faithful to forgive our unrighteousness and will put us back on track. Nehemiah 1:9 (NIV) says, *"But if you return to me and obey my commands, then even if your exiled people are at the farthest horizon, I will gather them from there and bring them to the place I have chosen as a dwelling for my Name."*

Tips for effective Obedience

- Be strict on the flesh and obey God.
- Tame the flesh and give it no voice where obedience to God is concerned. (Romans 13:14).
- Trust God enough to launch into His will. Be assured in God like Abraham.
- Hold yourself in and allow God's Spirit to prevail over the force and voice of disobedience.
- Mutter and muster over what the Lord will have you do till it gets done.
- Resist all dissuading forces with God's Word by declaring and exercising your ability in Christ.
- Shut out fears and doubts. Give no attention to your weaknesses. Assert to fear that it has no room in you. That sin will not have dominion over you (Romans 6:14).
- Get into action without delay, not entertaining dissuasion to the instruction.
- Keep your spirit in subjection to the Word.
- Allow God to be the final Arbiter and Authority as you do His will regardless of prevailing or contending circumstance,

acting by faith, not by sight (sensory perception).

- Keep your mind made up to please God with your obedience rather than to disobedience and please the devil. Fight this good fight (1 Timothy 6:12). Be resilient; be determined and dogged in God's will. The three Hebrew boys were resolute in God's will, despite the fiery furnace and whether the Lord delivers them or not (Daniel 3:17-18).

- Remember that only absolute obedience and not partial obedience attracts absolute reward.

- Obedience will increase your wisdom and understanding. The fear of the Lord (in doing His will) is the beginning of wisdom (Psalm 111:10). The Bible says wisdom is the principal thing. So, pursue wisdom and understanding by obeying so as to remain in God's will for a fulfilling life (Proverbs 4:7-13).

- Do it bravely or even rather afraid than not do it at all. The Bible advises not to cast away our confidence which has great recompense of reward (Hebrews 10:35). Take that leap into God's will. He will take charge of you, honour and reward your obedience. His Word says to cast your cares upon Him for He cares for you (1 Peter 5:7).

- Deal with every Word of God like the Person of God (John 1:1) for God's Word is God. His Word is truth and life; it never fails (Psalm 119:160, John 14:6).
- Do not just be a reader or hearer of the Word of God; be a doer; practice and carry out the Word (James 1:22).

"Now therefore hearken unto me, O ye children: for blessed are they that keep my ways. Hear instruction, an*d be wise, and refuse it not. Blessed is the man that heareth me, watching daily at my gates, waiting at the posts of my doors."*
Proverbs 8:32-34

Conclusion

"In conclusion, be strong in the Lord
[be empowered through your union with Him];
draw your strength from Him [that strength which
His boundless might provides]."
Ephesians 6:10 (The Amplified Bible)

To be obedient to God is power; it is wisdom and life to those who live by it. John 6:63 says, *"It is the spirit that quickeneth; the flesh profiteth nothing: the words that I speak unto you, they are spirit, and they are life."*

Obedience implies reaching out to receive the outstretched hand of the Father and walking in line and along in His will for His purpose. The purpose of God is revealed in our lives when we obey and we are delivered from darkness, bondage and death. When the Father directs in His love for us, wisdom makes us receive (obey) it for our own benefit and advantage. Nehemiah 1:5 (NIV) says,

"Lord, the God of heaven, the great and awesome God, who keeps his covenant of love with those who love him and keep his commandments."

Doing what God wants us to do as instructed in His Word or as spoken directly to our spirit results in fruits of righteousness being produced in us. In obedience to God, you discover that you can never be disadvantaged. To disobey is costly (1 Samuel 15). The more we are responsive in obedience, the more acquainted we get with God's ways.

Psalm 119:102-105 says, *"I have not departed from thy judgments: for thou hast taught me.103 How sweet are thy words unto my taste! yea, sweeter than honey to my mouth! 104 Through thy precepts I get understanding: therefore I hate every false way.105 Thy word is a lamp unto my feet, and a light unto my path."*

In Proverbs 7:1-2 The Word of God admonishes us; *"My son, keep my words, and lay up my commandments with thee. 2 Keep my commandments, and live; and my law as the apple of thine eye."*

In 1 Kings 17:1-5, we see Elijah, a product of daring obedience, irrespective of the instruction and regardless of how daunting the instruction was, did as he was told: *"And Elijah the Tishbite, who was of the inhabitants of Gilead, said unto Ahab, As the LORD God of Israel liveth, before whom I stand, there shall not be dew nor rain these years, but according to my word. 2And the word of the LORD came unto him, saying, 3Get thee hence, and turn thee eastward, and hide thyself by the brook Cherith, that is before Jordan. 4And it shall be, that thou shalt drink of the brook; and I have commanded the ravens to feed thee there. 5So he went and did according unto the word of the LORD: for he went and dwelt by the brook Cherith, that is before Jordan."*

Elijah did accordingly, obeying God's direction and plan even with absolute confidence, trusting that God is able. It can only be confidence and trust in God that makes a man obey God like this. Blessed be God who is so faithful to those that trust in Him. It is expedient that we obey God even when it does not make immediate sense to us; as obeying God in any situation will always eventually amount in amazing results.

In Acts16:6 the Holy Spirit forbade the Apostles from going to Asia to preach, a good cause but reason for that at that time was best known to God. So when faced with instruction to carry out either from the written Word of God the Bible (2 Timothy 3:16), or received through our spirit (Ezekiel 3:24) or through audible voice (Matthew 3:17), it is important that we have confidence in God and obey, as it is our perception of God that determines our actions.

How do you perceive God? 2 Chronicles 20:20 says *"... Believe in the Lord your God, so shall ye be established; believe his prophets, so shall ye prosper."*

We see a profound statement made by Mary the mother of Jesus at the first miracle Jesus performed which was recorded in John 2:1-11: *"And the third day there was a marriage in Cana of Galilee; and the mother of Jesus was there:2 And both Jesus was called, and his disciples, to the marriage.3 And when they wanted wine, the mother of Jesus saith unto him, They have no wine.4 Jesus saith unto her, Woman, what have I to do with thee? mine hour is not yet come.5 His mother saith unto the servants, Whatsoever he saith unto you, do it.6 And there were set there six waterpots of stone, after the manner of the purifying of the Jews, containing two or three firkins apiece.7 Jesus saith unto them, Fill the waterpots with water. And they filled them up to the brim.8 And he saith unto them, Draw out now, and bear unto the governor of the feast. And they bare it.9 When the ruler of the feast had tasted the water that was made wine, and knew not whence it was: (but the servants which drew the water knew;) the governor of the feast called the bridegroom,10 And saith unto him, Every man at the beginning doth set forth good wine; and when men have well drunk, then that which is worse: but thou hast kept the good wine until now.11 This beginning of miracles did Jesus in Cana of Galilee, and manifested forth his glory; and his disciples believed on him."*

Faith, confidence and trust in God inspired Elijah to obedience which did not disappoint him; he was truly cared and catered for from point to point. 1 Kings 17:6-9 says, *"And the ravens brought him bread and flesh in the morning, and bread and flesh in the evening;*

and he drank of the brook. 7And it came to pass after a while, that the brook dried up, because there had been no rain in the land. 8And the word of the LORD came unto him, saying, 9Arise, get thee to Zarephath, which belongeth to Zidon, and dwell there: behold, I have commanded a widow woman there to sustain thee."

It was the same faith, confidence and trust that inspired Paul's obedience that he was so bold and audacious to accomplish all he did. Psalm 128:1-2 says, *"Blessed is every one that feareth the LORD; that walketh in his ways. 2For thou shalt eat the labour of thine hands: happy shalt thou be, and it shall be well with thee."* Paul was not intimidated by pressure or persecution but determined in complying with the will of God (Acts 20:21-24). Obedience empowers us, because as we believe God to do as He will have us, the Spirit of the Lord enables and empowers us for greater accomplishment.

Obedience will sort us out in any situation. The moment we put the Word of God to work by doing, the miracle begins; there will eventually be a way that brings joy and fulfillment because true fulfillment comes from true obedience. After obedience the blessings follows (Deuteronomy 28:1-9).The Lord assures the Israelites of the reward of obedience in these verses. The blessings of obedience are many. Every father will be pleased with an obedient child. The child's obedience confirms his respect and love for his father which provokes a father's blessings. In turn, the child also enjoys the love and favour of his father. God as our Father blesses us and makes our ways spectacular when we honour Him with our obedience.

Proverbs 16:7 says, *"When a man's ways please the* Lord, *he maketh even his enemies to be at peace with him."* In John 14:23 *"Jesus answered and said unto him, If a man love me, he will keep my words: and my Father will love him, and we will come unto him, and make our abode with him."*

Obedience keeps the presence of the Father with us. King Saul lost the presence of God by disobedience (1 Samuel 15:24-26).

Proverbs 29:25 says, *"The fear of man bringeth* a snare: but whoso *putteth his trust in the*

Lord shall be safe." Putting the will of man above God's will implies disaster. Proverbs 13:13 adds, *"Whoso despiseth the word shall be destroyed: but he that feareth the commandment shall be rewarded".* In Luke 6:26 Jesus said, *"Woe unto you, when all men shall speak well of you! for so did their fathers to the false prophets."* Meaning that we must be guided and not allow the voice of men to dictate or decide for us above God's word.

By obedience we hear to do God's Word so we are not just hearers. By hearing and also putting to action, the Bible says we are blessed (James 1:25). This is when we allow the Word to be the basis for our lives, propelling us in line with divine purpose. Mark 4:24 says, *"And he said unto them, Take heed what ye hear: with what measure ye mete, it shall be measured to you: and <u>unto you that hear shall more be given.</u>"*

As we hear to do, the blessing of hearing and doing becomes apparent in us. Matthew 7:24-27 says, *"Therefore whosoever heareth these sayings of mine, and doeth them, I will liken him unto a wise man, which built his house upon a rock:25 And the rain descended, and the floods came, and the winds blew, and beat upon that house; and it fell not: for it was founded upon a rock.26 And every one that heareth these sayings of mine, and doeth them not, shall be likened unto a foolish man, which built his house upon the sand:27 And the rain descended, and the floods came, and the winds blew, and beat upon that house; and it fell: and great was the fall of it."*

Obedience is a vital key to God's blessing for the extra-ordinary and the supernatural. Perfect obedience does not consider the circumstance but takes action based on confidence and commitment. In times when you find your obedience challenged, comfort yourself at such times with the peace you derive in surrendering to God's will other than to self or to the flesh. Submitting means to cast your cares upon Him, regardless of the means to obedience; as the fear of the Lord in you will back up your response of obedience into blessings and fulfillment. Deuteronomy 32:4 (NIV) says, *"He is the Rock, his works are perfect, and all his ways are just. A faithful God who does no wrong, upright and just is he."*

Remember that God's plans and thoughts for us are thoughts of good and not of evil as we obey regardless. As a good soldier for Christ, the Bible says to endure hardness (2 Timothy 2:3). We are to take our obedience to an exceptional level like Jesus as our example, resisting all hindrances along our ways unto outright obedience.

Hebrews 12:1-2 says, *"Wherefore seeing we also are compassed about with so great a cloud of witnesses, let us run with patience the race that is set before us, 2. Looking unto Jesus the Author and Finisher of our faith; who for the joy that was set before Him endured the cross, despising the shame, and is set down at the right hand of the throne of God."*

For our obedience to be outright and rewarding (Galatians 6:9), our reaction to the word of God must be absolute. God honours full, resolute and complete obedience. By partial obedience there is no submission as you are having your way, compromising God's way which can be dangerous. Partial obedience is as disobeying because it errs in the God-aim; dishonouring God's arranged plan. Wisdom is obeying God wholly.

Proverbs 2:1-12 says *"My son, if thou wilt receive my words, and hide my commandments with thee; 2 So that thou incline thine ear unto wisdom, and apply thine heart to understanding;3 Yea, if thou criest after knowledge, and liftest up thy voice for understanding;4 If thou seekest her as silver, and searchest for her as for hid treasures;5 Then shalt thou understand the fear of the Lord, and find the knowledge of God.6 For the Lord giveth wisdom: out of his mouth cometh knowledge and understanding.7 He layeth up sound wisdom for the righteous: he is a buckler to them that walk uprightly.8 He keepeth the paths of judgment, and preserveth the way of his saints.9 Then shalt thou understand righteousness, and judgment, and equity; yea, every good path.10 When wisdom entereth into thine heart, and knowledge is pleasant unto thy soul;11 Discretion shall preserve thee, understanding shall keep thee:12 To deliver thee from the way of the evil man, from the man that speaketh froward things."*

Jesus is a great example in obedience, on the night before crucifixion, He prayed: *"... nevertheless not My will but Thy will be done."* (Luke 22:42). Jesus, facing an agonising death was determined to walk in obedience with the Father's will. Luke says that Jesus was in such anguish over His decision that night. *"And being in agony he prayed more earnestly: and his sweat was as it were drops of blood falling to the ground."* (Luke 22:44).

Jesus, just like us, *"....was in all points tempted like as we are, yet without sin."* (Hebrews 4:15). To disobey is to sin. Jesus was exposed to the rudiments of life just as we are but excelled in pleasing the Father unto all obedience. He went through the painful but purposeful will of the Father without resistance, hesitation nor withdrawal. He offered Himself in submission so that the work of obedience can be perfect. If we can envisage Jesus as human who lived here on earth under the same life circumstance as ours, of flesh and blood (Hebrew 2:14), born as baby (Luke 2:7), scolded by his parents (Luke 2:48), who grew in wisdom and stature (Luke 2:52). He loved (John 11:5), experienced anger (Mark 3:5), was tired and sleepy (Luke 8:23), He wept (John 11:35) was betrayed (Luke 22: 48), He faced temptation (Matthew 4:1-11) and pain, felt forsaken and in anguish (Matthew 27:46), He bled (John19:34) and still being as able to perfectly fulfill the will of the Father.

Jesus Himself assures us in John 14:12 *"Verily, verily, I say unto you, He that believeth on me, the works that I do shall he do also; and greater works than these shall he do."* These greater works include obedience regardless of its cost.

If we profess Jesus as Lord of our lives, it means we have surrendered all to Him, which is the totality of our being in full submission in acquiescence to His will. The Bible says He keeps His covenant of Love to those who obey Him (Deuteronomy 7:9).

God gave these Words to the Israelites in Leviticus 20:22 (NIV): *"Keep all my decrees and laws and follow them, so that the land where I am bringing you to live may not vomit you out."*

It is important that we keep and follow God's instruction to lead us into His 'Canaan land' and promises for us. To disobey is to derail from the path of God's plan for us. It is by the fulfillment of God's Word that we can be fulfilled. As we observe in the last scripture, we do not want to be vomited out of God's particular plan for us as individuals but rather to be in His perfect will.

Leviticus 26:3-4 says *"If ye walk in my statutes, and keep my commandments, and do them; 4 Then I will give you rain in due season, and the land shall yield her increase, and the trees of the field shall yield their fruit."* We have to obey God before we can access His promise. The Word of God is for acting upon in order to activate the blessing inherent in it.

Obedience stirs Heaven's blessing into operation according to your desires too, just as you have acted in obedience according to God's plan. One thing we must note is that if we do not obey God we are either obeying man or the devil, implying sin and destruction. God in His mercy would rather that all men come to the knowledge of the truth. He is faithful, merciful and unwilling that any should perish (1Timothy 2:4). God is ever willing to help us in our weaknesses. Ezekiel 36:26 *says, "A new heart also will I give you, and a new spirit will I put within* you: and I will take away the stony heart out of your flesh, and I will give you a heart of flesh." What is required is to call on Him with a genuine repentant heart for change that it may be said of us too as said of David in Acts 13:22, "...I have found David the son of Jesse, a man after mine own heart, which shall fulfil all my will."

Words for our inspiration

"All scripture is given by inspiration of God, and is profitable for doctrine, for reproof, for correction, for instruction in righteousness: That the man of God may be perfect, thoroughly furnished unto all good works." (2 Timothy 3:16-17)

"By faith Abraham, when he was called to go out into a place which he should after receive for an inheritance, obeyed; and he went out, not knowing whither he went." (Hebrews 11:8)

"My son, give me thine heart, and let thine eyes observe my ways." (Proverbs 23:26)

"Great peace have they which love thy law: and nothing shall offend them." (Psalm 119:165)

"If ye be willing and obedient, ye shall eat the good of the land." (Isaiah 1:19)

"I will never leave you nor forsake you." (Hebrews 13:5b)

"All things work together for good to them that love God." (Romans 8:28)

"Trust in the Lord with all thine heart; and lean not unto thine own understanding. In all thy ways acknowledge him (by obedience), and he shall direct thy paths." (Proverbs 3:5-6)

"For I know the thoughts that I think toward you, saith the Lord, thoughts of peace, and not of evil, to give you an expected end." (Jeremiah 29:11)

"Humble yourselves (in obedience) therefore under the mighty hand of God, that he may exalt you in due time." (1 Peter 5:6)

"...he (Jesus) humbled himself, and became obedient unto death..." *(Philippians 2:8)*

"If ye abide in me, and my words abide in you, ye shall ask what ye will, and it shall be done unto you." *(John 15:7)*

"Be ye therefore followers of God, as dear children." *(Ephesians 5:1).*

"Whoever despises the word and counsel [of God] brings destruction upon himself, but he who [reverently] fears and respects the commandment [of God] is rewarded." *(Proverbs 13:13 Amp)*

"For if these things be in you, and abound, they make you that ye shall neither be barren nor unfruitful in the knowledge of our Lord Jesus Christ." *(2 Peter 1:8)*

"And now, brethren, I commend you to God, and to the word of his grace, which is able to build you up, and to give you an inheritance among all them which are sanctified." *Acts 20:32*

Hymn

When we walk with the Lord
In the light of His Word
What a glory He sheds on our way!
While we do His good will
He abides with us still
And with all who will trust and obey

Trust and obey
For there is no other way
To be happy in Jesus
But to trust and obey

*"Now the God of peace, that brought again
from the dead our Lord Jesus, that great
shepherd of the sheep, through the blood
of the everlasting covenant, Make you
perfect in every good work to do his will,
working in you that which is wellpleasing
in his sight, through Jesus Christ; to
whom be glory for ever and ever. Amen."*
Hebrews 13:20-21

Prayer for a heart of Obedience

Dear Lord, I surrender all to You that I may walk in obedience and be worthy of You. I ask that by grace I constantly overcome the weakness of the flesh to disobey.

I pray that I may constantly walk in the path of obedience so that I may fulfill Your designed purpose for my life unto all pleasing.

Thank You for the Holy Spirit my Helper and Guide into Your perfect plan for me.

This I pray in Jesus' Name. (Amen).

Special Note

- To disobey instruction is to embrace destruction.
- Obedience will liberate, elevate and celebrate the obedient.
- Keep impressing God with obedience and He will keep increasing you in blessings.
- To obey is to be upheld
- Obedience makes you hear God more.
- Keeping in tune with God requires keeping in line with Him.
- Intimacy with God demands our into His will
- Obedience accrues obeisance.

"Let us hear the conclusion of the whole matter:
Fear God, and keep his commandments:
for this is the whole duty of man."
Ecclesiastes 12:13
King James Version (KJV)